- In nine months, net pioneer Candice Carpenter saw her net worth change from $100 million to nine hundred thousand dollars.

- The human genome project was finished four years ahead of schedule.

- Entire categories of beverages (wine coolers, unusual teas, designer vodkas) gain significant market share and then fade to zero—in a matter of months.

- In nine months, Napster went from zero to 10 million users. Nine months later it had 50 million users (the most successful technology introduction of all time) and was essentially out of business. (And as I write this, it's back again!)

- The most popular shows on network TV are in formats that didn't even broadcast in prime time three years ago.

- A little-known scientist in Scotland cloned a sheep.

- Dell Computer was one of the most profitable growth stocks of the 1990s. Quarter after quarter, year after year, Dell piled on growth and profits. Now, the CEO of Dell warns that the future is murky. The stock is stagnant at best.

- Scout Electromedia burned through more than $20 million in venture capital and then closed—all in less than 120 days.

- The price paid by marketers for Web traffic dropped 99 percent over a ninety-nine day period.

- The media went nuts over a new invention that turns out to be a scooter.

- Last year seven thousand new grocery products were introduced. The average large grocery store stocks thirty thousand items.

The harder we work, the less we accomplish.
The more things change, the more we lose.
The more time and money we invest in one strategy,
the more turbulent our market becomes,

$f\mathbf{P}$

Survival Is Not Enough

Zooming, Evolution and the Future of Your Company

Seth Godin

Foreword by Charles Darwin

This edition first published in Great Britain
by Simon & Schuster UK Ltd, 2002
A Viacom Company

1 3 5 7 9 10 8 6 4 2

Simon & Schuster UK Ltd
Africa House
64–78 Kingsway
London WC2B 6AH

www.simonsays.co.uk

Simon & Schuster Australia
Sydney

A CIP catalogue record for this book
is available from the British Library

ISBN 0–7432–2122–2

Printed and bound in Great Britain by
Omnia Books Ltd, Glasgow

SIXTEEN YEARS AGO, I picked up a book by Tom Peters. In a caffeine-induced frenzy brought on by a particularly bad day at work, I read it in one sitting and a light bulb went on. A whole new set of ideas filled my head and changed the way I looked at work—forever.

I had the same experience when I first read *Fast Company*. And then again when I discovered Peppers and Rogers. It happened with Jay Levinson, Malcolm Gladwell and Zig Ziglar, too. Big ideas don't gradually sneak up on you . . . they just arrive, fully formed cosmologies, ready to go.

This book is dedicated to all the smart people who have turned lights on for me.

contents

Contents

Evolution is a fact, not a theory.

As many more individuals of each species are born than can possibly survive; and as, consequently, there is a frequently recurring struggle for existence, it follows that any being, if it vary however slightly in any manner profitable to itself, under the complex and sometimes varying conditions of life, will have a better chance of surviving, and thus be naturally selected. From the strong principle of inheritance, any selected variety will tend to propagate its new and modified form.

If we look to long enough periods of time, geology plainly declares that all species have changed; and they have changed in the manner which my theory requires, for they have changed slowly and in a graduated manner.

I can see no limit to this power, in slowly and beautifully adapting each form to the most complex relations of life.

Companies that can evolve slowly and constantly will triumph.

Natural selection can act only by taking advantage of slight successive variations; she can never take a leap, but must advance by the shortest and slowest steps.

No winning strategy lasts forever.

No fixed law seems to determine the length of time during which any single species or any single genus endures.

And most companies will disappear.

More individuals are born than can possibly survive. A grain in the balance will determine which individual shall live and which shall die,—which variety or species shall increase in number, and which shall decrease, or finally become extinct.

The good news is that you can teach old dogs new tricks.

Our oldest cultivated plants, such as wheat, still often yield new varieties; our oldest domesticated animals are still capable of rapid improvement or modification.

The bad news is that competition is cutthroat.

The struggle almost invariably will be most severe between the individuals of the same species, for they frequent the same districts, require the same food, and are exposed to the same dangers.

Companies that zoom have a competitive advantage.

The modified descendants of any one species will succeed by so much the better as they become more diversified in structure, and are thus enabled to encroach on places occupied by other beings.

Alas, there are no guarantees.

But which groups will ultimately prevail, no man can predict; for we well know that many groups, formerly most extensively developed, have now become extinct.

People have trouble embracing these facts because they're hard to see in real time.

The chief cause . . . is that we are always slow in admitting any great change of which we do not see the intermediate steps . . . The mind cannot possibly grasp the full meaning of the term of a hundred million years; it cannot add up and perceive the full effects of many slight variations, accumulated during an almost infinite number of generations.

Survival Is Not Enough

MORE THAN SURVIVAL

IT'S 3:00 A.M., AND IT'S HOT. I can't sleep. My laptop can't reach the Internet through the overburdened phone system here at the Cleveland Holiday Inn. Frustrated, anxious and exhausted, I jump in my car and drive the deserted streets of northern Ohio.

Around the corner, I pass a Kinko's. The lights are on. They're always on. I walk in to find hundreds of thousands of dollars of electronics, all just waiting for me. Color copiers, fax machines and an entire room full of fast computers with a T1 connection to the Internet. Five minutes and twenty dollars later, I've checked my mail and printed out a memo. Time to get some sleep.

But I can't get to sleep. I sit up for hours, wondering about that Kinko's.

How did Kinko's grow from one tiny store in California all the way to an all-night home office in Cleveland? (Turns out there were eight within sixteen miles of my hotel.) It took a couple of decades, but the company grew and changed and expanded—

almost like an organism, spreading across the country until it had filled every niche it could find.

At the same time that Kinko's was growing, dozens of its competitors were silently shrinking, disappearing, becoming extinct.

Look at the development of any business and it's bound to be surprising. Surprising in how unplanned, irregular and random it is. Some businesses grow and ooze and morph and expand, others reach a certain spot and freeze. Why do some companies thrive while other companies, though similar, fade away? I knew that there must be a pattern and a dynamic behind all this apparent chaos, but I was having trouble finding it.

I've been fascinated with the work of Charles Darwin for a long time, and it occurred to me that companies were very much like species. They were changing and evolving right before our eyes. However, unlike animals, companies fret about this change so much it makes them miserable.

Why is there so much pain in our business lives? It's almost as if people were taking Charles Darwin at his word, focusing on "survival of the fittest" instead of something more than that. If all you do at work is hope to survive, your day can't be much fun.

We're all working too hard. Putting in more hours than we'd like, nervous about the future, uncertain about our roles and our goals. We work too hard to hope for mere survival. Our goal must be to thrive and prosper, not just get by.

Darwin writes extensively about extinction. We don't want to grapple with the idea that our company is about to become extinct. No one wants to become extinct, but the alternative—change—is hard. Going through all of the uncertainty and hassle to barely survive (or worse, become extinct) doesn't seem fair.

We don't know how to talk about change and **evolution**. We know it's here and it's real and it's essential and it's painful, but we don't have the words for it. I believe that there's a goal beyond survival, that we can actually thrive and find joy in working with all the chaos that surrounds us. That we can look forward to change and turbulence as an opportunity to increase our success. My hope is that this book will give you the words to describe these phenomena as well as an understanding of how they work.

There is no secret spell or closely guarded incantation. The solution is written down everywhere you look, from the park to the zoo to the checkout at your local grocery store. And the idea that evolution can work in business is not news, either. Jack Welch and GE have been doing it for years, and will be happy to teach you about it.

So why doesn't everyone use this successful approach? Because we have a genetic reflex to avoid change. The secret of this book is that your success is not going to be due to your plan. It's the process you use that matters.

I'm proposing a pretty radical way of thinking about business, but one that's nothing new to an evolutionary biologist. As a result, there are a lot of oddball terms and occasional side trips to go on as you read these pages. I hope you'll bear with me, because the end result is a totally different set of glasses you can use to look at your job, your career, your company and even the companies you invest in. (See the author's note at the end of this book for a full and complete disclaimer about scientific accuracy.)

If you try to stuff these ideas through the filter of the way you work today, they won't make sense. This is a very different sort of paradigm for what companies do all day, and it requires a different posture and approach.

My goal in writing this book is to explain the paradigm and sell you on why you ought to run your business with it. The tactics will reveal themselves as you head down the path to a brand-new kind of organization.

The benefits are simple: less stress at work, less chaos in your daily life and occasionally, if you're lucky, a landslide success that pays off big-time.

Once you have the words, I'm confident you'll find ways to let the power of evolution go to work. When it does, you'll discover that you can create explosive group and personal success that can further transform your company.

Most of us view change as a threat, and survival as the goal. Change is not a threat, it's an opportunity. Survival is not the goal, transformative success is. It's thrilling if you give it a chance. This book contains an idea about ideas. An ideavirus about change, one I hope you will find worth spreading.

The Paul Orfalea Story: A Process, Not a Plan

One of my favorite entrepreneurs is a guy named Paul Orfalea. Paul is brilliant and quite successful, but he's unbelievably modest and also very honest about his shortcomings.

Paul is profoundly dyslexic. He didn't learn how to read until he was well into elementary school and did nothing in high school that would be associated with the idea of success. He went to college but didn't care an awful lot about his classes. It was the perfect background for an entrepreneur.

Paul started a little copy shop (so little he had to wheel the machine outside to make room for customers) on his college campus. He sold pens and paper and made copies. That store grew to become Kinko's, a chain with more than one thousand outlets that he was able to sell for more than two hundred million dollars to an investment group.

The secret to Kinko's success is disarmingly straightforward. "My reading was still poor and I had no mechanical ability, so I thought that anybody who worked for me could do the job better,"

Paul explains. He set up a unique co-ownership structure that let him grow the business with more flexibility than a franchise could offer. The end result is that for years, Kinko's stores were partly owned by someone local.

Paul described his job to me this way, "I just go from store to store, see what they're doing right and then tell all the other stores about it."

By allowing local entrepreneurs to make millions of low-cost experiments every year (just three per day per store gets you to that level) and then communicating the successful ones to the other stores, he was able to set the process in motion that led to that all-night store I found in Cleveland. The Cleveland store wasn't part of a specific plan, but it was very much the outcome of a specific process.

Very little specialized knowledge is required to open a copy shop. Yet Kinko's dramatically outpaced every other competitor by reinventing what a copy shop was, every single day. Kinko's did

---

"I just go from store to store, see what they're doing right and then tell all the other stores about it."

---

not have a patented new technology. Instead, it had a posture about change that treated innovations and chaos as good things, not threats.

The more successful Kinko's got, the more likely it was to get job applications and coventure deals with people who made the company even more successful. The more Kinko's stores there were, the more likely it was that people would seek one out. The better Kinko's did, the more successful it became.

Kinko's became a success. Working there was fun because the company attracted people who could compound its growth. Kinko's stopped worrying about surviving and enjoyed the ride.

It's interesting to see that since the takeover of Kinko's by an investor group, new management has bought out the individual owners and installed a command and control system. Kinkos.com is regrouping and the entire chain is experiencing slower growth, despite external economic and technical conditions that should have allowed it to grow even faster.

Paul was right. All of us are smarter than any one of us.

Survival Is Not Enough: The Summary

1. Change is the new normal. Rather than thinking of work as a series of stable times interrupted by moments of change, companies must now recognize work as constant change, with only occasional moments of stability.

2. If you and your company are not taking advantage of change, change will defeat you.

3. Stability is bad news for this new kind of company. It requires change to succeed.

4. Change presents new opportunities for companies to capture large markets. Change is the enemy of the current leader. Change also represents opportunities for individuals to advance their careers.

5. Companies that introduce products and services that represent significant changes can find that they lead to rapid, runaway successes.

6. Companies that cause change attract employees who want to cause change. Companies that are afraid of change attract employees who are afraid of change.

7. Many employees fear change. Fear of change is rational—after all, it can lead to bad outcomes. But now, not

changing is more likely to lead to a bad outcome than changing!

8. Management can't force employees to overcome their fear of change through short-term motivation.

9. By redefining what change is, companies can change the dynamic of "change equals death" to "change equals opportunity."

10. The way species deal with change is by evolving.

11. Companies can evolve in ways similar to those used by species.

12. Companies will evolve if management allows them to.

13. There are three ways that species evolve: **natural selection, sexual selection** and **mutation**.

14. Companies can do the same thing by using **farmers, hunters** and **wizards** to initiate changes in their organizations

15. Companies that embrace change for change's sake, companies that view a state of constant flux as a stable equilibrium, **zoom**. And zooming companies evolve faster and easier because they don't obstruct the forces of change.

16. Once you train the organization to evolve regularly and effortlessly, change is no longer a threat. Instead, it's an asset, because it causes your competitors to become extinct.

17. Many CEOs reject evolution and do whatever they can to stop it.

18. If your company is too reliant on your **winning strategy**, you won't evolve as quickly.

19. A runaway success occurs when a **positive feedback loop** reinforces early success.

20. **Fast feedback loops** teach you what's working and—more important—get you to change what's not.

21. Everyone in your company can work to reinvent what you do in parallel, dramatically increasing the speed of innovation within the company.

22. Low-cost, low-risk, real-world tests are the most likely to have high return on investment.

23. Your company's posture regarding the process of change is far more important than the actual changes you implement.

24. If you have employees who don't embrace this posture, they will slow you down and cause you to make bad decisions.

25. A company that zooms will attract zoomers, allowing it to enter **runaway**, dramatically increasing its advantage over its competitors in a changing environment.

To help you manage the new terms that appear in this book (in **boldface** the first time they appear), you'll find a glossary with more details at the end.

Chapter 1

CHANGE

> Change is out of our control, and the way we deal with change is
> outmoded and ineffective Our organizations assume that we live
> with a different, slower time cycle.

Guillotine or Rack?

My first job was cleaning the grease off the hot-dog roaster at the
Carousel Snack Bar, near my home in Buffalo. Actually, it wasn't a
roaster. It was more a series of nails that rotated under a light
bulb. I also had to make the coffee and scrub the place clean every
night. It very quickly became obvious to me that I didn't have
much of a future in food service.

I didn't have to make many decisions in my job. And the manager of the store didn't exactly look to me to initiate change. In
fact, she didn't want anyone to initiate change. (My suggestion
that we branch out into frozen yogurt fell on deaf ears, as did my
plea that it would be a lot cheaper to boil hot dogs on demand than
to keep them on the rack under the light bulb all day.)

Any change, any innovation, any risk at all would lead to some
terrible outcome for her, she believed.

After I set a record by breaking three coffee carafes in one shift,
my food-service career was over. I was out on the street, unem-

ployed at the tender age of sixteen. But from that first job, I learned a lot—and those lessons keep getting reinforced.

Just about every day, I go to a meeting where I meet my boss from the snack bar. Okay, it's not really her. But it's someone just like her: a corporate middle-person who's desperately trying to reconcile the status quo with a passionate desire to survive. My boss didn't want to jeopardize her job. She viewed every day and every interaction not as an opportunity but as a threat—a threat not to the company but to her own well-being. If she had a mantra, it was "Don't blow it."

In her business, she faced two choices: to die by the guillotine, a horrible but quick death, or to perish slowly on the rack—which is just as painful a way to go, if not more so, and guaranteed to leave you every bit as dead. But in her nightmares, only one of those two options loomed large—the guillotine.

I have to admit it. I have the same dream.

Have you ever spent a night worrying about what your boss (or your stockbroker or a big customer) is going to say to you at that

---

"In her business, she faced two choices: to die by the guillotine, a horrible but quick death, or to perish slowly on the rack—which is just as painful a way to go, if not more so, and guaranteed to leave you every bit as dead."

---

meeting the next morning? Have you ever worried about some impending moment of doom? That's fear of the guillotine.

But almost no one worries about the rack. We don't quake in our boots about a layoff that's going to happen two years from now if we don't upgrade our computer systems before our competition does. We're not afraid of stagnating and dying slowly. No, we're more afraid of sudden death, even though the guillotine is probably a far better way to die.

For a long time, I was angry with my old boss and the people like her. I was upset that they were living through so much pain. Most of all, I was frustrated that they were slowing the pace of change at their companies. Now I realize that I was wrong. It wasn't her fault. She couldn't help being frantic and stressed. She didn't want to be that way. Management made her do it. They made her do it with their policies. With their inspection systems. With the command and control mindset that prevented her from making changes she knew were right.

Nobody likes change.

Real change, earth-shattering change, stay-up-all-night-worrying change isn't fun. At most companies, it's a huge threat, an opportunity for failure, a chance to see the stock plummet, to watch divisions get axed, to hear customers scream and yell. Our companies are organized as big machines, designed to resist big change at every turn.

The problem is that today we don't have a choice. We can't leave innovation to the small guys, the startups that have nothing to lose. Either we change our businesses, or they die.

Frantic at Work?

Companies aren't organized for change. They've never needed to be. Growing and profiting from stable times was a terrific strategy.

Forced into an era of rapid change, the response of companies organized for a stable environment is to ask managers and employees to act as a buffer between the company and the changing outside world. Alas, it's not working.

Are you working longer hours than you used to? Most people do. And along with the long days, it often feels as if your day is filled with one emergency after another. We spend so much time putting out fires and nervously anticipating the next crisis that there's almost no time left to do our real jobs.

While it's easy to find the reserves to deal with a temporary crisis (in fact, you might even enjoy the adrenaline rush that comes with a deadline) we can't keep this up forever. Accountants can deal with April 15 because they know it only comes around once a year. It's a temporary emergency. Unfortunately, being frantic at work is no longer a temporary phenomenon. Change is

> "We can't work more hours. We can't absorb more stress or endure more anxiety at work. We can, on the other hand, radically redefine what we do at work and create organizations that are designed to succeed regardless of what our ever-changing future produces."

now constant, and the fundamental ideas we have built our companies and our careers upon are going out of style fast. They're disappearing so fast that for the first time, you have to deal with the implications of change instead of waiting for a retirement, a promotion or a new job. The world is changing on your watch, and it's not fun.

Somewhere along the way, it was decided that it was our job to absorb the stresses that come with change. Our job to work longer hours, take more personal risks, absorb more stress. Your frustration and stress aren't atypical. They are, however, unnecessary.

We can't work more hours. We can't absorb more stress or endure more anxiety at work. We can, on the other hand, radically redefine what we do at work and create organizations that are designed to succeed regardless of what our ever-changing future produces.

Your job shouldn't be to stand between your company's old rules and the new rules of the outside world. Instead, your company needs to change from the inside out. Your company needs to learn to zoom.

A company that zooms embraces change as a competitive opportunity, not a threat. A company that zooms is responsive to new opportunities and doesn't freeze in the face of an uncertain future.

Every company zoomed when it was young. But success has spoiled most organizations, and they're now too fat, too stuck and too afraid to zoom again. If your company is under stress, it only has two choices. Either it changes or it requires people like you to absorb the stress. The first is productive, energizing and profitable. The second leads to an unhappy frenzy.

Because the chaos we're facing came to us gradually, it's easy to believe that we can gradually adapt in the way we deal with it. It's not true. The way we used to do business—dependent on highly profitable physical goods and manageable cycles of change—is over.

In *Permission Marketing*, I wrote about a major shift in the power between consumers and marketers. In the old days, marketers were in charge. They controlled how and when they communicated with consumers. We built our entire consumer culture around the idea that repeated television and print advertisements could profitably entice consumers to spend money. Businesses that invested in interrupting people became incredibly profitable. Marketers were in charge. They controlled the marketplace and consumers were sheep. Those days are over. Businesses can no longer manage consumer attention, consumer attention manages them.

In this book, I'm making a much broader argument. In the old days, companies were in charge. Good managers managed change. They controlled how and when a company would respond to the outside world. Those days are over. You can't manage change. Change manages you.

If you're unhappy, stressed, tapped out and/or losing money in our chaotic world, perhaps it's time to consider a radically different approach. It's possible to build a company that embraces change instead of fighting it. A company that attracts people who want to move fast, not slow. A company that changes faster than its environment, creating one landslide hit after another.

Businesses That Don't Change Are in Danger

Winners change; losers don't. Digital, Wang, Western Union, Compaq, Penn Central, PointCast, Infoseek—all are on my list of losers, because all of them hesitated and lost huge opportunities. Every one of them was king of the hill until they toppled off, all the while struggling in vain to make the world stay the way it was.

Federal Express is different. Talk to David Shoenfeld, former vice-president of worldwide marketing and customer service for FedEx, and sooner or later, ZapMail comes up. About fifteen years ago, someone at FedEx got the bright idea of putting very expensive fax machines at key FedEx offices and having those offices act as middle-persons for same-day fax delivery. They put David in charge of it. A big promotion for him at the time. Alas, ZapMail was a giant failure. By the time FedEx pulled the plug on it, ZapMail had reportedly cost the company as much as $300 million.

You'd think that would have cured FedEx's management of the urge to embrace change—that forevermore, whenever someone came up with a business-busting idea, someone else would mention ZapMail, and people would roll their eyes and walk away. You know what? The people at FedEx do exactly the opposite. They're damn proud of ZapMail, of their willingness to take risks, of the mistake that proved their willingness to change.

At the Carousel Snack Bar, I learned three lessons that are just as valid now, twenty four years later, as they were then. The first is that you should never take a job that requires you to bring your own grease rag to work. Second, jobs in which you don't initiate change are never as challenging, fun or well paid as those in which you do. And third, companies that don't change, vanish (my snack bar is now a shoe store).

It's easy to see those lessons at work on the Net, but change isn't just about the Internet. When the Internet is old news, companies will still be turning over. Remember DeSoto and Pierce-Arrow and Dusenberg and Packard and American Motors? How about Borland and Spinnaker Software and Ashton-Tate and (almost) Apple? Or A&M Records? Or Orion Pictures?

Is it possible to change too often? We all know someone like crazy Uncle Kenny, who has had forty different schemes over the last forty years. Juice bars, day trading, vitamins, carpet cleaning-Kenny is always changing. I don't think we're in any danger of becoming Uncle Kenny. There's a difference between flitting and changing, and most of us know the difference. Anyone who's been through the death of an industry knew what to do. They just weren't able to do it.

Change Is the New Normal

"Excellent firms don't believe in excellence—only in constant improvement and constant change." That is, excellent firms of tomorrow will cherish impermanence—and thrive on chaos.

Tom Peters, *Thriving on Chaos*, 1987

In the first chapter of *Thriving on Chaos*, Tom Peters rolled out a litany of turbulence that was hitting the world fifteen years ago. He wrote about Chrysler buying AMC, GE buying United Technologies, Hyundai's entry into the U.S.A., the influx of IPOs, the wild ride of People Express Airline, the craziness in the packaged-goods industry and the marvel of Minit-lube.

Peter Drucker and other long-term thinkers would have us believe that every generation believes that it, and only it, is undergoing massive change. After all, we survived the Industrial Revolution, two world wars, the atomic bomb and *Gilligan's Island*. Surely today's change is no more radical than the changes we've already worked our way through.

Computers and the networks that connect them are the reason that today's change is fundamentally different from the changes business has survived before. Change in a connected world always has more repercussions. Now, change leads to more change. Turbulence spreads. Bob Metcalfe, the inventor of Ethernet, coined a law that still stands: The power of a network increases with the square of the number of computers (or people) hooked up to it. Two people with a fax machine is interesting. Two hundred million people with e-mail changes the world.

Fifty years ago, a recession in Tangiers wasn't felt in Tampa for years (if ever). Today, it takes minutes. When Tom Peters wrote about constant change fifteen years ago, he was feeling the beginning of a computerized marketplace. But there were no networks then. No Internet. No wireless. No computerized stock trading.

Today, **entropy** rules. It's as much a law of the new economy as it is a law of science: Things rarely become orderly on their own. As Stephen Hawking has pointed out, while it's possible for a cup to fall off a table and break into a million pieces, it's pretty unlikely that those million pieces will ever leap back onto the table and reassemble themselves into a cup.

Systems, of course, can fight entropy. People know how to take a bunch of random springs and turn them into a watch. The sun "knows" how to take a series of random solar flares and tame them into a coherent source of heat and light. While the world we're talking about is an organic system, that doesn't keep random acts from occurring. And they're occurring as often as they used to.

Now, though, it's worse. Far worse. Because when a cup falls off that table, it affects every cup in the world. Which means that, like snow and rocks joining an avalanche, changes are happening far more often than they used to. Now we have to deal with their changes, not just our changes.

There have been four significant structural changes in business over the last twenty years. These changes mean that we're not in the same boat we were then. They mean, instead, that we're facing permanent adjustments to the status quo:

1. The speed at which we make decisions is now the factor that limits the speed of business. It's our decisions that are on the critical path for getting things done. The lead time for many of the things we need to do (from starting a company to getting a shipment of leather) has shrunk. Everything in the company waits—not for a shipment or a process, but for a decision.

2. The Net has made information close to free and close to ubiquitous, further fueling the need for speed. And we can deliver that information digitally, which means it doesn't degrade with distance or handling.

3. A provincial worldview created islands of stability. Those islands are disappearing. There's only one market, and it's the whole world.

4. Metcalfe's law (networks get more powerful when they connect more people) has reached infinity. The invasive network of phones, faxes, e-mails and the web now connects virtually all of us.

In 1987, Tom Peters sensed an unraveling that continues to this day. Except it's getting more pronounced and there is no turning back. Change is the new normal, and organizations will either embrace this or fade away.

What Happens When the Jaguars Die?

I was reading *The New York Times* a few months ago and I came across an op-ed advertisement from Greenpeace. The headline read, "What happens when the jaguars die?"

Not being particularly concerned with jaguars, I turned the page and continued reading. But after a few minutes, my curiosity wouldn't let go of the question. What did happen? So I turned back and read the ad.

Jaguars, it turns out, live in Mexico. Their favorite food is rabbits. And when jaguars die (due to encroachment on their habitat by people), the rabbits multiply like, well, rabbits. And when the number of rabbits dramatically increases, the grassland turns to desert. In other words, a small change in the status of one animal (the jaguar) can lead to millions of acres becoming a desert.

The ecosystem is very responsive. Kill off one crop and entire species that depend on it become extinct—just like the ecosystem your business operates in. A small change—say the availability of competitive pricing data to your customer base—can have implications for the way your company must run all of its operations in order to succeed. For example, the commercial printing business is no longer driven by local printing shops and friendly salesmen. Because a client can discover what a job ought to cost, every printer (whether online or off) must respond to a dramatically different landscape.

Unstable ecosystems are the enemy of traditional businesses, especially market leaders. Market leaders have optimized a plan for extracting the maximum value out of the ecosystem as it is *today*. When the ecosystem changes, not only does the company lose its ability to extract that value, but the size of the company actually begins to work against it.

So, if you are going to make bets about the future of the ecosystem in which your company finds itself, do you feel comfortable betting that the system will stay stable? In 1963, the Bucyrus-Erie Company built the largest electric stripping shovel ever built, designed to extract coal from its mine in Kansas. This device was so large (it was 160 feet tall and weighed more than 9 million pounds) that it had to be built on site and from the beginning was designed to live and die on that one patch of land.

The ecosystem for cheap coal mining in Kansas in 1963 was stable enough that Bucyrus-Erie felt it was a safe bet to invest the millions of dollars the device cost. This is the same reason it's so easy to buy an airplane from Boeing—just about any commercial bank on earth will give you a loan, taking just the plane as collateral. The banks are confident that no one is going to invent something that makes that plane obsolete any time soon.

But how many ecosystems are as stable as coal mining or aircraft? Ten years ago, no one would have bet against NBC or Merck or Sunbeam or Mary Kay Cosmetics or Knight Ridder. Yet today, the future of all of these companies is up for grabs.

The Problem with Factories

Ever since we got serious about farming and factories, business-people have embraced the idea that investments in physical plant will pay off. Go to a meeting at Universal Pictures and they'll happily show you the back lot. Visit my dad's hospital crib factory and you'll see punch presses and paint lines. Harvard University has stately ivy-covered buildings. Random House is erecting a huge skyscraper in midtown Manhattan.

At the very heart of capitalism is the idea that an entrepreneur can take money from investors and spend it on infrastructure that will pay dividends for years to come. Having a bigger, better factory was always the best way to get rich.

There are two big problems with factories, though. The first is that in times of rapid change, infrastructure ceases to be an advantage and begins to be a drag. Keeping those factories busy and paying dividends often forces a company to hold back on innovation.

The second problem is that the really profitable companies no longer rely on factories. Since 1970, the average weight of a dollar's worth (inflation adjusted) of exports from the United States has dropped by 50 percent. In other words, we're shipping ideas, not stuff.

If a factory doesn't need to be near the end user (because of cheap shipping) and doesn't need to be near the client (because of

---

"Being factory-centric doesn't increase your profits, it decreases them."

---

the ease of long-distance communication), then location is not really a competitive advantage. A factory owner often finds himself in the commodity business.

As I write this, I'm enjoying music from a group called Timbuk 3, based in Atlanta. The CD was manufactured by a Japanese company, in Indiana, and is being played on a Korean CD player through an amplifier made in Washington state. Finally, the music comes out of 150-pound solid-marble stereo speakers made in Thailand (which have tweeters that were made in Denmark).

My guess is that at every step along the way, the "manufacturer" had a choice of factories he could use to make each component. And he probably didn't own them.

Do we still need factories? Of course we do. How else are we going to make all this stuff? My point is that while the world still needs factories, that doesn't mean you have to own them. Owning a factory will probably become a profitable niche business, a way to make a nice living. But fast-moving, high-growth, zooming companies don't need to own them.

Because factories are no longer local, because the ultimate provider is no longer the manufacturer, the model that was factory-centric is dead. Being factory-centric doesn't increase your profits, it decreases them. Being factory-centric doesn't *decrease* your time to market, it *increases* it.

What's the Internet Got to Do with the Chaos?

This is not a dot-com book. A year ago, the Internet was going to undo all that was done and change everything that needed to be changed. Old ideas like profit and loss and revenue were obsolete and we had better get used to a very different economy. Control-top.com (yes, it was a real company, and yes, they sold control top pantyhose) and others of its ilk were somehow going to rewrite the rules of economics.

Now that we've all lived through the much-heralded correction, there is a new chorus of voices. That chorus reminds us that it was all hype, that things are now back to normal and that the voices of change were wrong, wrong, wrong.

As with most dialectics, the future is somewhere in the middle. The Internet is changing everything, but the changes are going to be less visible than we expected. Consider this postcrash (March

2001) statement from *The New York Times*: "The Internet, with its myriad online connections, speeds the transmission of ideas, good and bad, and simplifies their reach. It has allowed business managers to peek into every link of the supply chain that feeds their manufacturing processes, and to change direction with a nimbleness that would have been unimaginable just a few years ago." The article is about eight thousand people at Solectron losing their jobs (in one day).

In the old days, Solectron could have taken a year or more to adapt and adjust to a slowdown in the economy and the market for circuit boards. Now, with every company connected to every other, it takes minutes, not months or years, for the bad news to trickle in. In many ways, the **supply chain** is now as turbulent as the stock market. And companies that are at the end of that chain can get whipsawed all day long.

There used to be slack in the systems that connect companies to one another. It took a long time to tally up the orders, a long time to deplete inventory, a long time for the purchasing department to figure out what the sales department was doing. All that slack is now being sucked out of the system. The networking of every department means that the guys in purchasing can find out about a sales slowdown within minutes, not months.

The Internet is the reason that change is piling up exponentially. The Internet is the reason that this chaos is not like all the chaos that came before. Not because of one-click shopping at Amazon.com or searching for Turkish cab drivers on Yahoo! No, because the Internet connects every company and every consumer in an instantaneous web, where response times approach zero.

Successful Businesses Hate Change

In stable times, businesses succeed when they get very good at something. Maximizing their ability to act like factories—factories that take in raw materials and money at one end and spew out products and services at the other—is the secret to success.

Since the start of the Industrial Revolution, the goal of most companies has been to grow in size and to become more efficient as they do. These companies work to stamp out variability in the products they make, to avoid risk, to be reliable, predictable and scalable. They invest in infrastructure and policy manuals to reduce variability and increase efficiency.

In changing times, however, the rules appear to be quite different. What worked in stable times is precisely what will lead to a company's demise when things are changing. Rather than being big and efficient and risk-avoiding, it appears that the companies that do best (in the long run) in times of change and volatility are small in size and risk-taking in profile. Efficiency takes a back seat to guts (and luck). The policy manuals have actually become a hindrance.

Change is nothing new. Even stable companies lived with change. But it was like gravity—it was always there, it was predictable and we could deal with it. Even the change was stable!

We now live in turbulent times. Everything in our world—from marketing to technology to distribution to the capital markets—is changing faster than ever (and not always in the same direction). Yet most companies are clueless about what's causing the change, how the change might affect them, and more important, what to do about it.

The company stock is falling, but we do nothing until it's too low. Then the board fires the CEO, the new CEO conducts massive layoffs and the company limps along until someone buys it. Or we see a new technology revolutionizing one industry after another, but ignore it and hope it will go away before it gets to us. One day, it does get to us, and our competitor uses it to trounce us with a breakthrough new product.

Successful businesses hate change. People with great jobs hate change. They abhor confusion and chaos and shifts in the competitive environments. Market leaders seek out and cherish dependable systems.

But upstarts and entrepreneurs love change. Turbulence scrambles up the pieces on the game board and gives them a chance to gain market share and profits. And since there are always more competitors than market leaders, there's a huge demand for change. More innovation. More competition. More change. *It's not going to go away. It's going to get worse.*

Stable times force us to think of our companies as machines. They are finely tuned, easy to copy and scale and own. We build machines on an assembly line, following specific rules and focusing on how to make them cheaper and with ever-better reliability.

If your company is a machine, you can control it. You can build another one, a bigger one. You can staff the machine with

---

"Our organizations are not independent machines, standing in the middle of a stable field. Instead we work for companies that are living organisms. Living, breathing, changing organisms that are interacting with millions of other living, breathing, changing organisms."

---

machine operators, and train them to run the machine faster and faster.

In times of change, this model is wrong. Our organizations are not independent machines, standing in the middle of a stable field. Instead, we work for companies that are organisms. Living, breathing, changing organisms that are interacting with millions of other living, breathing, changing organisms.

Managers and employees are looking for a way to make sense of this turbulence. We need a metaphor to help us not merely deal with external change, but *embrace* it in order to succeed.

This is not business as usual. It's a new principle that is going to feel unnatural at first. We will need a new vocabulary to even discuss it. Borrowing from the field of evolutionary biology, I am going to try to outline a new definition of a successful business. We need to reinvent what it means to lead (or work in) an organization.

The Promise of Positive Feedback Loops and Runaway

Surviving change is a noble goal, but what if embracing change didn't just help us survive but actually gave us better results?

Before working your way through the rest of the book, where I describe a different way of dealing with change, consider the upside. Instead of forcing you to put out fires and deal with emergencies, it's possible for change to present you and your organization with mammoth new opportunities.

Scientists talk about positive feedback loops. These are systems in which the inputs are amplified and become the outputs—and then go right back in and become the inputs again. That screeching sound that comes from a poorly designed microphone is called feedback because amplified sound from the microphone comes out of the speakers and goes right back into the microphone. Positive feedback loops can have beneficial outcomes, however.

Money in the bank encounters a positive feedback loop like the one in this graph because you earn interest on your money, and then interest on your interest and then ever more interest on that interest.

An avalanche starts on the top of a mountain, with just a few

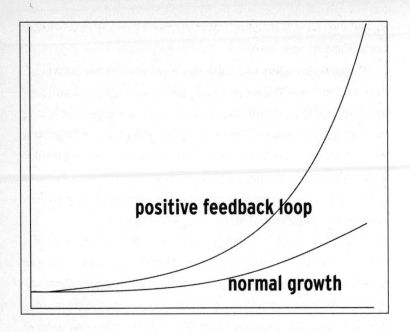

positive feedback loop

normal growth

rocks falling off a precipice. But each rock starts a few more rocks rolling, and the avalanche increases in force until it is powerful enough to wipe out an entire village. This is a positive feedback loop.

A company succeeds in large part because it's successful. An early lead becomes an insurmountable lead, because the early advantage is itself a factor in the company's success.

As markets become more chaotic, they create opportunities for new players to grab an early advantage. With planning and luck, that advantage can turn into a huge lead, especially if a positive feedback loop reinforces that lead.

When people start interacting with each other in a positive feedback loop, the loop gets amplified, entering a stage called runaway. The evolutionary science pioneer Sir Ronald Fisher coined this term for an evolutionary system that races ahead, faster and faster, reinforced by sexual selection.

We're all familiar with the runaway phenomenon. A book starts selling, and suddenly, people start to buy it *just because other people are buying it*. People sell items on eBay because that's where all the buyers are. But all the buyers are there because sellers know that's where to find them!

Of course, runaway can work in the other direction as well. A stock on the NASDAQ starts to fall, which leads to news and gossip about the fall, which leads to even more investors panicking and selling their shares. The stock's price will decrease faster and faster, with investors fleeing and bargain hunters buying until it finally reaches equilibrium again—sometimes at just 10 percent of what the stock was originally worth. This feedback loop sucked all the money out of the stock.

During the Great Depression, many banks closed because of a run on the bank. Consumers have confidence in a bank as long as there's plenty of money on deposit and they believe that other consumers also have confidence. But once lines started to form outside the bank, previously unpanicked investors started to have second thoughts. After all, they thought, if everyone on this line gets their money back, there might not be enough left in the vault for me. Of course, if no one had felt this way, then there wouldn't be a line in the first place. As soon as some people start to have second thoughts, though, it reinforces the fear across the population, making the problem worse and amplifying it through a positive feedback loop of negative thinking.

The marketing department would like your company to be fast enough to launch products that can take advantage of these positive feedback loops. Your CFO wants a company nimble enough to pile onto these successes, because it can transform your stock into a runaway hit.

Runaway Can't Last Forever—Nothing Does

Cisco is a fine example. It established itself early on as the leader in Internet infrastructure. This meant that investors seeking to make a bet on this sector invested in the company, which drove up its stock. The increasing stock price gave Cisco a currency (a valuable stock) that it could use to buy other companies. In the last decade, it acquired hundreds of companies, which further reinforced its position as the leader, which attracted more investment and further drove the stock price up.

Cisco stock peaked at eighty dollars a share. According to the *New Yorker* columnist James Surowiecki , that gave the company a valuation that assumed that the company would be bigger than the U.S. economy is today in just twenty-five years. Runaway had led people to want to buy Cisco at any price, ignoring the obvious fact that no company can grow forever at the speed of Cisco's early years. Once the market realized that mass hysteria had set in, the stock dropped more than 80 percent in a runaway decline.

Despite the limits on runaway, Cisco returned an astonishing 89,000 percent (that's not a typo) increase in its stock price during the 1990s. Good work if you can get it! Runaway can't last forever, but it's fun while it lasts. If you can figure out how to trigger a runaway, you may be able do it again, creating a never-ending series of runaway successes.

The Best Form Of Runaway Is the Least Obvious

There's a positive feedback loop that can change your company and the way it deals with change. Your company can attract a different sort of employee and create a runaway organization.

I flew on TWA last week, and the entire experience was exhausting. The people behind the counter, beaten down by years of working for a company on the edge of bankruptcy, seemed tired. The planes, way behind on cosmetic maintenance due to a lack of investment, seemed tired. The flight attendant, who had stuck with the airline because she had seniority, seemed tired. By the time I got home, I needed a nap.

What sort of person applies for a job at TWA today? Is it someone who wants to embrace change, move quickly and take risks? I doubt it. TWA is reinforcing its factory view of the world every time it hires someone.

Compare this negative feedback loop with the one that was in place at Kinko's for years. What sort of person applied for (and got) a job as a manager at Kinko's? The company was able to reinforce its ground-up approach to change in the people it hired. The more zoomers they hired, the more likely they were to zoom. Unfortunately, new management is doing its best to eliminate the zoomers (they fired most of the kinkos.com division where the highest concentration of zoomers worked) and go to a factory-centric model.

If you were a hotshot networking engineer during the 1990s, the obvious place to go to work was Cisco. If you were an entrepreneur building a networking company during the 1990s, the obvious place to sell your company was Cisco. Great people want to work for fast-growing companies. The power of this positive feedback loop is underrated, though. Just as markets gravitate to leaders, so do employees. And smart employees in a hurry are the building blocks of your future success.

The Evolution Alternative

Now that we've seen the impact the changing environment is having on our organizations (and more important, on us), let me lay out a very different point of view. The rest of this book describes in detail this alternative way of doing business.

As I've described, change is out of our control, and the way we deal with change is outmoded and ineffective. Our organizations are built on the assumption that we live with the slower time cycle of yesterday. We build factories and try to make them perfect.

If we try to control something that is out of our control, we're going to fail. The failure is going to lead to frenzy, to stress and ultimately, to the demise of our organization.

Perfect is impossible when there is rapid change, and thus we're forced to search for a different way and a better metaphor. Smart businesses can learn from animals, which respond to competition in the environment through evolution.

Evolution (real evolution—inheritable modifications over many generations) is the most powerful tactic available to us for dealing with change. Organizations and individuals can put this proven organic technique to use by permitting change to occur, not fighting it.

A mutation is a mistake or random feature created when a gene or an idea is transferred. By finding positive mutations and incorporating successful new techniques into a company's makeup, organizations can defeat their slower competitors. It is our fear of changing a successful **winning strategy** (the tactics we use to succeed) together with our reliance on command and control tactics that combine to make us miserable.

There's a different way. We start by bypassing our fear of change by training people to make small, effortless changes all the time. I call this zooming. Then we can build a company that zooms and that attracts zoomers. As the company gathers steam, it will enter runaway, distancing itself from its competitors and dominating markets by embracing the change that will inevitably come.

Chapter 2

WHAT EVERY CEO NEEDS TO KNOW ABOUT EVOLUTION

As change continues to create more turbulence, organizations can learn from animals, which respond to competition in the environment through evolution.

Evolution—inheritable modifications over many generations—is the most powerful force we have for dealing with change.

EVOLUTIONARY BIOLOGY is endlessly fascinating, but there isn't room to go into a lot of detail here. Instead, I'm going to assert the essential facts as I see them because they provide an essential analogy to how business can not only survive but flourish in times of change.

If you want to explore the evolution connection more thoroughly, an expanded version of this chapter is available for free by writing to evolution@zoometry.com. My computer will automatically send you the free bonus chapter and then your e-mail address will be automatically deleted from my system.

Competition Drives Change

Two backpackers are finishing up a long trip through the Canadian Rockies. As they turn a corner, they come upon a small family of grizzly bears, including two cubs. Mother grizzlies are notoriously protective, so the two backpackers don't wait around. They immediately turn and start running, with the angry grizzly in hot pursuit.

After a few hundred yards, one backpacker turns to the other. "Stop," he gasps. The other stops for a second, staring incredulously

---

"When there is competition, there is evolution."

---

as the first puts down his pack and starts taking off his hiking boots. As his friend sees him putting on his running shoes, he yells, "What are you, crazy? You're never going to be able to outrun that grizzly, even with sneakers on!"

Finishing his lacing, the first backpacker stands up and starts jogging away. "I don't have to outrun the grizzly. I just have to outrun you."

Evolution isn't benign. If you're a panda, there's competition from your brothers and sisters for food. There's competition between species. There are predators that would be delighted to have you for lunch. And there's a changing habitat as well.

Over time, the organisms on earth have faced cataclysmic changes. Ice Ages. Meteors. Onslaughts by dinosaurs, plagues and lava. Entire continents moving, valleys flooding. And throughout the entire process, one thing remained constant: when there is competition, there is evolution.

The Big Ideas

There are six ideas that I'd like to share from evolutionary biology:

1. Every time an organism mates, the genes from both parents are shuffled and combined. This reshuffling is the

action that creates new organisms and allows evolution to proceed. This is the only time the genes get changed, but it happens every time. Try as the organism might, it can't change its genes.

2. Genes cause offspring to resemble their parents.

3. Genes that are successful are more likely to spread through a population.

4. The choice of which genes are passed on to future generations is influenced by three factors: sexual selection, natural selection and mutation.

5. Evolution is a bottom-up phenomenon, with each gene and each organism driving the process. Elephants don't need permission from the chief to mate.

6. Organisms that reproduce more often are more responsive to changes in the environment. Fruit flies survive change better than tigers.

What's a Meme?

A glimpse at the last hundred years of human history is all you need to see that our society is evolving at a rapid clip. Everything from technology to clothes to the way we organize our companies has changed quite a bit over time. While our bodies continue to evolve slowly, something is happening to our ideas. It seems as though a second type of evolution is occurring.

Human beings carry huge brains, far bigger as a percentage of body size than almost any other creature. Some evolutionary biologists believe that our big brains came from sexual selection. Women were more likely to mate with men who could make conversation or share gossip or paint a picture. The end result was offspring with still bigger brains.

Our brains, in other words, worked just like the tails on a peacock. The more fit a human was (healthier, better evolved to compete in the environment), the more resources he could put into brain development. As Geoffrey Miller wrote, women went for big brains. (Men get a say as well, and it appears that they went for big brains too.)

This created a positive feedback loop. It reinforced a runaway increase in the size of the human brain. Male offspring inherited big brains, females inherited both big brains and an attraction to men with big brains. This created a mammal (us) whose brain is way out of proportion to our size.

A million or more years ago, memes were used by our genes as a way of advertising the health and size of our brains (and thus our bodies) in much the same way as moose grow big antlers. Men (and women!) who were good at creating and passing on memes were more likely to get their choice of mate and have children who often inherited the skill.

For a long, long time, we didn't do much with our brains. We used them to find mates, but we didn't use them to enhance our survival by building huts or spears or laundromats.

Years after our brains got bigger, we increased our ability to play with more abstract ideas. We learned to imitate, to communicate, to pass along the ideas that occurred to us. Richard Dawkins calls these ideas "**memes**."

A meme is a unit of innovation (an idea), the same way a gene is a unit of physical heredity. It's a rule or a concept or an idea that can be spread from one person to another, much as a gene can be passed down from parent to offspring. There are big memes and little memes and memeplexes and all manner of confusing meme terminology.

Here are some examples:

The macarena was a meme. It spread when someone insisted

you get up and do a line dance with a crowd of people. This was a particularly virulent meme—it ripped through the population in a matter of months. Then it faded away and died.

Shaking hands is a meme as well. The people you meet can shake hands with you perfectly well, despite the fact that they may not know how the tradition arose, why they're doing it or how you prefer to do it. It's an idea that has been communicated around the world, and it's transferred from person to person when we're quite young.

Recipes are a meme. Once someone figures out an amazing recipe for **crispy tofu**, he can write it down and give it to anyone else who knows how to cook. That person ought to be able to make tofu with almost exactly the same result.

Once the meme is immortalized in a cookbook, it spreads far and wide and becomes part of the **meme pool**. It becomes part of the catalog, the foundation of memes that people who know how to cook rely on. Variations like crispy tofu parmesan, of course, would be built on the foundation of the original crispy tofu meme.

My book *Unleashing the Ideavirus* was a set of memes about how ideas spread. The book itself became a popular memeplex, spreading by e-mail to more than a million computers. Because the e-book version was free, it was easy for people to spread the meme. It moved, intact, from person to person.

My last example is the evolution of the Corvette. Go to www.auto.com/newmodels/qchist6a.htm and you will see pictures of the cars many of us grew up with. It's obvious that it would have been impossible for General Motors to have launched the 2000 Corvette in 1955. Not only was the technology too primitive to produce that car, but the audience would have refused to buy it.

At every step along the way, each Corvette altered its memes to respond to the competitive (and fashion) pressures of the day. In turn, the memes used by Corvette created new competitive pressures on every other car manufacturer. Dramatically faster than genetic evolution, the **memetic evolution** of the Corvette is obvious to anyone looking at the last thirty-five years of development of that car.

Because the pace and impact of meme creation increases when there are more memes to compete with, it's a self-reinforcing positive feedback loop. Thus, with each passing day, we're reinforcing our ability to create and pass along ideas (and unlike peacock feathers, memes are working for both sexes). Like the avalanche and the best-selling book, there's a positive feedback loop in place for memes, and they've entered runaway.

Memes compound the runaway effect because unlike moose antlers, they can morph and grow and spread quite quickly. Memes are unbelievably aggressive compared to genes. While the genes that make a moose's antlers big have to wait for another generation to roll around before they can be improved through sexual selection, memes are busy improving themselves daily. The Internet, of course, is the best thing that ever happened to memes,

---

"The speed of memetic evolution is now the speed of our evolution. The faster we can spread and change memes, the faster our systems evolve."

---

because it further accelerated their velocity and cut the length of a meme "generation." Which leads to even more runaway.

The speed of memetic evolution is now the speed of our evolution. The faster we can spread and change memes, the faster our systems evolve.

Memetic evolution is a neat idea. Ideas evolve over time, just like species. Those ideas are made up of the building blocks of ideas (memes) just as organisms are driven by their genes. As we'll see, memes can evolve very quickly, but they don't always.

Memes Are Not the Same As Genes

At times, the analogy gets pretty tortured.

Genes, for example, make up DNA, a standardized structure for their transfer. Memes have nothing similar. More important, genes all have a similar data length. It's easy to look at a strand of DNA and say, "that's a gene." Memes, on the other hand, often include other memes. We can say, "Memes evolve," but we can't say, "Genes evolve." It's not clear what the smallest unit of a meme could be, nor what the largest is. Even the precise definition of a meme is in dispute.

A meme doesn't exist without a sympathetic human brain to understand it, while a gene is an independent entity. Memes don't get shuffled during reproduction as genes do, either.

Unlike genes, memes get stuck. This is where the challenge of paradigm shifts come from: Human beings build a memeplex around a core meme (the sun revolves around the earth) and then, when the core meme is shown to be untrue, we have a great deal of trouble dealing with all the changes we're going to have to make in the secondary memes that surround the meme that changed. We essentially have to build a whole new memeplex.

With all of these deficiencies, why bother talking about memes at all? I think the most important reason is that memes are the driving force in our evolution. And since we know a lot about how species evolve genetically, we can take that understanding and apply it to the way our ideas and organizations change over time. Memes give us a way to apply our knowledge of genetics to the new sort of evolution that people and their organizations are experiencing.

Periodicity in Memes

How do memes change over time?

If there is a valid analogy between genes and memes, then we need to understand the periodicity of meme change. Species evolve by shuffling their genes every time they reproduce. We measure generations because the creation of offspring is the seminal moment in the evolution of a species. Memes don't have offspring, though. So, if there isn't a reshuffling at birth, then where is the periodicity?

In the picture below, the circles represent cars without airbags. The triangles are cars with airbags installed. The black box is the process that surrounds the design, creation and purchase of a car—natural selection (does this feature make the car sell better than the competition?), sexual selection (does this feature encourage executives at other car companies to include it in their cars?) and mutation (did this feature get added somewhere in the production process?).

By representing car purchases as a box (labeled NSM for natural selection, sexual selection, mutation), we can illustrate the way a population looks as it changes:

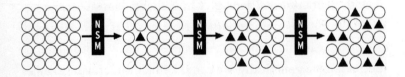

As long as cars with airbags are more fit for the environment than the cars without them, more triangles will enter the population. As older cars get replaced, the percentage of the population with airbags will increase. As new cars are purchased, the chances that their manufacturers have adopted the airbag meme are greater, so it's more likely that these cars will have airbags.

The growth in the number of triangles is impressive, but what controls how fast it occurs? What kinds of populations spread a meme like this the fastest?

In the example above, we saw what happens in eight model years, with a population that buys a new car every two years. Over this period of time, the average person bought four cars.

What if people bought cars once a year instead of every other year? Then, in that same period, we would have eight generations, not four:

Of course, some cars stick around as used cars and some cars only last a few months at a rental car franchise, but that doesn't change the result of this illustration. A new meme spreads through a population faster when the periodicity is higher.

I'm cheating a bit here. Airbags are a special meme, embodied in a physical item (a car) that most people own sequentially—one at a time. Memes are far messier than genes. For that reason, we'll call the collection of memes in an organism mDNA to distinguish

"A new meme spreads through a population faster when the periodicity is higher."

it from the more elegant DNA that is at the heart of living beings. There's no standard mDNA-like strand that holds a certain number of memes and forces them to be in one state or another.

The greatest strength of memetic evolution is that we don't

have to give birth in order to recombine a set of memes. This means that memes can move and change far faster than genes. However, the very thing that makes memes move so quickly also impedes their movement.

Unlike genes, sometimes memes get stuck. Every time an organism reproduces, every single gene is up for grabs. All of them are randomly recombined, kept or discarded. While there are unfit genes still remaining in our genome (like cystic fibrosis), natural selection keeps them under intense pressure until they disappear.

Unfit memes, on the other hand, appear to be able to stick around for far more generations than unfit genes. Part of the reason memes are messier than genes is that people can willfully stick with a meme for their entire lives, and then pass the meme on to future generations. There is no absolute periodicity, no moment when all memes are up for grabs.

It's like a game of poker in which the dealer never has to shuffle the cards.

If a top-forty radio station updates its playlist every week instead of every month, new records will get played more often. If a chef goes back to cooking school every year, his food will change more often than that of a chef who has a huge stack of menus printed and never posts a special.

In shorthand, companies that zoom have a very high periodicity when it comes to memetic evolution. They shuffle the cards frequently, until they find a hand that they like. They don't fight the power of evolution, and that gives them an ever-increasing advantage.

Genes versus Memes

Genes want stability and safety. Genetic evolution is slow and it relies heavily on a biological transmission method that leads most offspring to be very similar to their parents. The more stable the environment, the more likely it is that an organism that's already evolved for a particular niche will thrive.

Genes don't care about the good of mankind. They care about themselves. Genes selfishly want to spread themselves by

---

"The best breeding grounds for memes are places filled with new challenges and multiple changes."

---

reproducing, creating descendants who will successfully pass on the genes.

Genes that get passed on the most are the ones that inhabit successful organisms. And organisms are most successful when the environment they evolved for works as they expected it to.

Animals are basically cowards. The genes they carry have been chosen for survival and **fecundity** (how likely they are to be passed on), and that means that they avoid dumb risks and scary environments. Given the choice, genes would prefer to live in the Garden of Eden forever. They know they'll have more offspring that way.

Like genes, memes are selfish. They don't care about the success of your company or the Catholic Church or the state of the Hudson River. They are different from genes in one critical aspect. They hate stability.

The best breeding grounds for memes are places filled with new challenges and multiple changes. The adoption of the Internet, for example, opened the way for tens of thousands of new memes about communication and business to spread widely.

In environments that are constantly changing, many people are open to a new idea, a new strategy, a new way to win. So we communicate more often, try new techniques, happily share our successes with others. It's in those environments that memes spread the fastest and have the most impact. Compare the memes racing through a high school on the first day after summer vacation with the still air in a centuries-old monastery.

Memes are spreading faster and faster (thanks to electronic media) and that just makes us hungrier for new memes. Human genes don't have a reinforcing positive feedback loop, so they are fairly stable. Our memes, however, are in a state of runaway and they appear unstoppable.

The conflict between genes and memes goes right to our very being. That fear you felt in the pit of your stomach the first time you raised your hand in business school is the best evidence I can offer you. Your genes got you this far by avoiding conflicts with the chief and other powerful competitors. But your memes desperately want to share a new idea and watch it spread.

There's no place that I know of where the conflict between genes and memes is more profound than in organizations. Work is what we call the place where the genes go to find food and to survive. And forever, the genes have driven us to work, obsessed with minimizing risk and finding enough food and resources to survive.

As we enter a new millennium, it appears that the memes have caught up with (and even passed) the genes. Work now belongs to our ideas and the way we manipulate them, with our genes destined to take a back seat—screaming as they go.

A positive feedback loop has been created for our memes. The more we create, the higher the stakes are for establishing ourselves as cutting-edge meme-creators. This leads to an ever-increasing growth spiral, in which people are constantly working to outdo the competition in creating more and more memes. It's risky and unstable and doesn't put food on the table every night. It's no wonder the genes hate it.

Denying Evolution Doesn't Make It Go Away

The simple engine of evolution—inheritable changes in the species, occurring over thousands of generations—is able to produce extraordinary results. No factory has ever produced anything as marvelous as a bird, yet the bird evolved from a simple single-celled organism, one step at a time.

Darwin felt that people had trouble visualizing anything that took place over the course of a hundred million years. These days, in a world where McDonald's aims to get you food in less than sixty seconds, that's even more true.

The increased power of the meme as an engine for intellectual evolution changes the discussion about time. We could go to the Galapagos and watch finches evolve over the course of a decade. But now we can sit at home and tune in to CNN and watch evolution happen before our eyes. Not the evolution that led to lemurs and porcupines, but the evolution that led to Pokémon cards.

In 1906, San Francisco suffered an earthquake and burned to the ground. Eleven years later, the entire city had been replaced. Why is it that it is easy for us to replace something that disappears or fix something after it breaks, but we are unable to improve what we are currently using?

In the two hundred years before the fire, San Francisco evolved. It went from seven wooded hills to a vibrant post–Gold Rush city. It evolved one step at a time. And then it was finished and it stopped evolving.

When there's a vacuum, new memes step in, solving the problem of the moment. After the earthquake, without a city to tear down, the people of San Francisco could focus on building a new one. An empty lot represents an opportunity for someone to imitate someone else's success (with modification), and the faster they do it, the more they will succeed. The developers of San Francisco did it quickly because each success led to new successes, with nothing to slow them down.

Business is now at a turning point. Memetic evolution is driving our companies to change faster and faster, yet most managers and CEOs do everything they can to keep their companies from evolving. They deny that evolution is a powerful force for change, rarely considering how it might help.

Every company I know of, from Kinko's to Starbucks to Viacom, became a success by evolving. They morphed and grew and changed until they became successful. And then each company willfully stopped evolving. They, like almost all successful companies, created roadblocks designed to slow evolution. They have policies and committees and investors. They've invested in factories and the people who run them. These roadblocks are fairly universal and they're built into the very fabric of their organization.

Penguins don't evolve on purpose. They don't have meetings about evolution. They don't debate the most effective routes for their future on the island. Instead, evolution is built into their daily lives and is embodied in their reproductive cycle. Because evolution is automatic, it happens whether the penguins find time for it or not.

The difference between a penguin and your company is simple: While you both evolved to the point where you could succeed, the penguin continues to evolve and your company tries desperately not to.

Your organization, unlike the penguin, is built on the fiction that someone is in charge, that the world is stable, that you get to choose what happens next.

Alas, change is unceasing and unyielding, so the best strategy is to embrace it and to evolve. To fight change is to fight a losing battle. To manage change is a hopeless task. To successfully evolve, however, is to win. Every time. You and your employees can consciously choose to evolve or not.

If you work for a company that doesn't look forward to change, that views change as a threat not an opportunity, then your com-

---

"The penguin continues to evolve and your company tries desperately not to."

---

pany is failing, and it's failing faster every day. You now have competitors that will get stronger from the turbulence, and over time, they will win.

Chapter 3

FEAR AND ZOOMING

Evolution is the best way for a species to respond to change. Organizations fight hard to stop evolution because they are afraid of change.

The way to permit evolution to do its work is to bypass our fear of change instead of trying to overcome it. Zooming helps us make small changes without fear.

Four Reasons People Freeze in the Face of Change

According to research reported in the *Psychological Bulletin*, there are four attributes that contribute to an individual freezing in the face of change. Take a look at this list and see if any of these four situations exist in your organization:

- Pressure from deadlines
- Fatigue
- Fear
- Bosses who desire closure, not uncertainty

If there's an established company in this country that doesn't face these four environmental factors every day, I've never encountered it.

Compare this to the attitude in many start-ups, especially those that are launched in a slow stealth mode (where people keep their day jobs) or by college students:

- The deadlines are private and not particularly expensive if missed.

- The employees have so much nervous energy that they fail to act fatigued.

- They are fearless because there's very little to lose.

- Their bosses are embracing uncertainty, because they don't have the faintest idea how to do things the "right" way. Trial and error becomes a business strategy.

The First Barrier to Change: Committees

If there are three people in a group, how many handshakes do you need before everyone is introduced and the meeting can start? The answer is pretty easy—it's three. If there are five people, the answer is ten. And if there are ten people, the answer is forty-five. Now Metcalfe's law kicks in again: For a hundred, you'll need 4,950 handshakes. And that's why big companies are so slow to process change.

In a start-up, if two or three people agree to try something, it

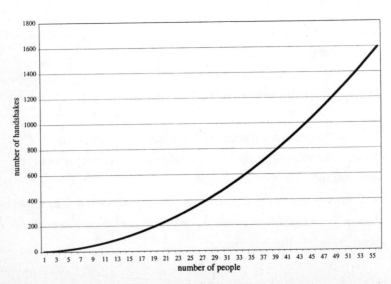

gets done. No need to smooth out all the rough edges or spend a lot of time defending the idea while you try to get buy-in from a large committee.

If there are ten people on a task force, however, you now need forty-five one-on-one meetings just to get everybody interacting. If Bob in accounting isn't happy with one element of your idea, it's easier to just leave that element out than it is to argue with him.

Most organizations make it easy for just about any committee member to say no to a change, but require a unanimous yes for anything to move forward. The bigger the committee, the longer it takes a meme to change.

The Second Barrier to Change: Critics

Why is it so hard to switch winning strategies in midstream? Why do we need entrepreneurs and venture capitalists and start-up companies to demonstrate to a big company what it knew already? Sometimes it seems as though the only way a big company can change is for a new company to start threatening its market. And often, by the time the big company realizes what's happening, it's lost its best chance for market domination. The big company may still win. But they would have won bigger if it had changed sooner.

Game theory gives us the best way of understanding why smart companies do dumb things. It's because the standard a successful

---

"The standard a successful company requires from a new winning strategy is far higher than the standard anyone else would ask for."

---

company requires from a new winning strategy is far higher than the standard anyone else would ask for.

The game theory is simple. If your company has success, the

cost of adopting a new strategy includes the cost of (at least conceptually) giving up the focus on that success. A competitor with nothing at stake faces less risk from the very same opportunity.

This leads to a phenomenon that's been little documented but crippling to many companies. Mark Henry Seibel calls it the humorous bazooka. It's the internal critic, the organized company culture of criticism that dooms most new winning strategies before they get a fair hearing. The term refers to the smiling coworker who shoots your new idea down with a carefully crafted joke. It hurts less than a direct rejection, but it's a rejection nonetheless.

If you live in fear of criticism, you're more likely to avoid taking risks that would invite criticism. Proposing an alternative to a winning strategy in a company that's successful is frightening, and most companies have a culture that supports the critic, not the new idea.

Internal corporate criticism takes many forms, most of them ill-informed and unfair. Here are five ways to be an unfair critic:

- Speak in absolutes. That film you saw last night is "the worst movie I've ever seen in my life." Heap as much negative thought in one sentence as possible.

- Criticize not just the item in question, but the background of the person or company responsible. If you can point out how much you disliked something else from this source, by all means do so.

- Criticize the motivation of the creator. Maybe they're doing it just for the money. Maybe they have some sort of secret political agenda. Better yet, the person behind it is certainly some kind of "wannabe"—a Robert Redford wannabe or perhaps a Dan Quayle wannabe.

- Criticize the taste and judgment of anyone who disagrees with your criticism.

- Make threats in your criticism. Threaten to "tell everyone" or to personally destroy the reputation or property of the creator.

Professor Teresa Amabile of Harvard Business School, in her paper "Brilliant but Cruel," tested a fascinating question: How do people decide if a person is smart? She showed the subjects in the experiment book reviews, some positive, some blisteringly negative. It turns out that the readers felt that the negative reviews were far more likely to be written by someone smarter than the person who wrote the positive reviews. In other words, negative thoughts equal intelligence.

In addition, most organizations make it easier to say no to a project than to approve it. If you say no, you don't have to justify your decision nor do you have to apologize if the project fails. If you say yes, you're going to have to work harder and take more risks, only to discover that your more conservative colleagues are more rewarded for saying no.

I think there are three criticism curses that make companies put the brake on innovation (and worse, put their best employees—the innovators—on the defensive):

- Successful companies fear external criticism.

- Successful innovators are more subject to harsh criticism.

- The less innovative employees of a company unfairly criticize the innovators.

At your company, this probably means that even though there are countless ways to take your early successes and leverage them into new successes, senior management is afraid to. It's afraid to take the risk of being criticized by customers, competitors or Wall Street. "We can't do xyz. We might fail!"

Telling someone not to be afraid of failing does little good. We *are* afraid of failing, and there's nothing much we can do about it. Except to redefine what failure is. Launching a product that

---

"We are afraid of failing, and there's nothing much we can do about it."

---

doesn't sell isn't necessarily a failure, especially if the alternative is never launching a new product at all.

Market Leaders Are Afraid of Failing

Why did the ubiquitous Howard Johnson's disappear? Why is Kraft so far behind in organic and nonengineered foods? Why did CBS wait for years and years before launching much of anything on cable or the Internet? Because market leaders are afraid.

Whether you work for JCPenney or Wal-Mart or Toyota or Ben & Jerry's, the company is going to be staffed with people who will be unfair (and harsh) critics of your new idea.

Why?

Because as companies mature and grow, they are far more likely to hire people to do jobs as opposed to hiring people who figure out how to *change* their jobs for the better. And those people are there because they embrace the status quo. They *like* their jobs. That's why they took them.

So, as a result, whatever you want to change has to be unfairly compared to whatever is happening now. And the comparison goes like this: *The worst possible outcome of what you're proposing* must be better than *The best possible outcome of what we're doing now.*

If Microsoft is good at anything, it's avoiding the trap of worrying about criticism. Microsoft fails constantly. They're eviscerated in public for lousy products. Yet they persist, through version after version, until they get something good enough. And then they can leverage the power they've gained in other markets to enforce their standard.

Most other companies don't get this chance to dominate one market after another. Back in the beginning, when they had nothing to lose, it was easy to launch an exciting innovation. But not now.

I've sat through some meetings that were absolutely surreal. Someone proposes an e-mail campaign that could dramatically increase a company's profitability and market share at the same time it would decrease customer service costs. Then the VP of customer service speaks up and says, "But what about the people who want to call us and end up getting this e-mail instead? What about them?" Now, simple math would show that she's talking about a tiny fraction of the audience. Worse, a quick audit would show that virtually *everyone* who calls in is upset by how long they have to wait on hold. So, while your proposal might offend a few customers, the critic ignores the thousands of customers who end up happier.

I'm not proposing that you run off and try whatever crazy idea pops into your head, ignoring constructive criticism that can make it better. I am asking, though, that before going into a meeting, your critics promise to follow these two rules:

- Criticize an idea based on how well it meets its objectives. If you don't like the objectives, criticize those separately.

- Fairly compare the idea to the status quo, warts and all. No fair accepting your current problems just because you already have them.

If you don't like the idea, it's your job to come up with something better by Friday. No solution is not a solution.

Change Equals Death

We're afraid of dying.

There's a good genetic reason for that. Organisms that don't fear death die more often than those that do. They throw themselves off cliffs, fail to store up enough food for the winter and engage in all sorts of dangerous activities. Death is a pretty good way to stamp out your genes.

As a result, organisms that are afraid of death are far more likely to live long enough to be able to reproduce, passing on their fear to their offspring.

In addition to genes that are afraid of death, we've evolved to carry genes that are afraid of change. Organisms that avoided situations filled with sudden changes were less likely to get killed and thus more likely to pass on that gene to their children.

It's not an accident that most species run away from the unknown. It's a successful strategy. Humans, in general, are no

"Organisms that avoided situations filled with sudden changes were less likely to get killed and thus more likely to pass on that gene to their children."

different. We fear situations filled with sudden, unexpected changes. This isn't a character flaw. It's human nature, and a large reason our species survived long enough for us to be here.

Very few people buy a coffin before they need one—even though it can save their estate thousands of dollars. Confronting our fears and accepting the inevitability of a bad outcome doesn't make us happy, so we try to avoid it.

According to one study, 38 percent of all workers are afraid that if they lose their job, they'll have trouble finding another one quickly . . . and 16 percent have withheld a suggestion for improving efficiency at work because they fear it will cost a coworker's

---

"Companies can evolve whenever they choose to."

---

job. With self-reported results like these (almost certainly low), the deep chasm of fear inside companies is obvious. People see change at work the same way they see death. It may be unavoidable but that doesn't mean you have to look forward to it.

But a great idea isn't going to kill you.

The spectacular difference between genes and memes is this: In order for a species to evolve, ancestors must become irrelevant and ultimately die. Genetic evolution happens in the future, not to you. You can't change your genes, you can only create the genes of your offspring. The best you can do is improve the species by having children with better genes. Those improved offspring take over after you're gone.

Memes, on the other hand, can evolve before our eyes, and do so without messing with our genes.

Organizations are nothing but collections of memes and the assets and people who implement them, so an organization can evolve without killing anyone. If a company had to wait for all of its employees to die or be fired before it could change, we'd live in a much slower world.

Instead, companies can evolve whenever they choose to. Bob Dylan can evolve every time he writes a new song. Enron can evolve when it decides to shift its focus from energy to data and financial markets.

Here's a new kind of change. A change that doesn't have to equal death. Memetics lets us manipulate ideas and processes and allow the organization to evolve without requiring us to die at some point. That means that the death of a meme is no big deal.

The death of a meme we're attached to is not the same as the death of one of our genes!

Why Change Management Doesn't Work

Two of the best change success stories of recent times are IBM and Corning.

IBM has managed to transform itself from a stodgy maker of mainframe computers and software into a services company, leading the way in a number of areas, from Internet infrastructure to chip design. During this same period, Corning went from a very sleepy manufacturer of glassware and plates into a high-tech champion, creating fiberoptic cables and high-tolerance ceramics.

Both changes, however, came with a fair amount of pain. Both companies were headed for disaster when strong leaders stepped in and forced the companies to transform themselves. While it worked in these cases, there are countless companies where the transition failed.

The leader of each company saw the problem and created an emergency. By declaring martial law, he was able to force people in the company to take action.

If a company doesn't start to react to outside change until it is in the midst of crisis, there probably isn't a choice. Its facing an emergency, and change management is the only option. But do companies have no choice but to wait until they face extinction, only to respond with panic?

IBM and Corning were lucky. They have great leaders *and* those leaders chose paths that worked. What if they had been wrong? If their last, best chance to change had been a failure, these once-great companies would have disappeared. This is what happened at Digital and Data General and Wang and thousands of other companies.

It's a little like plastic surgery. You can get a nose job, and your face will heal. But if you don't like the way your new nose looks, you can't head back into the operating room for yet another nose. Big, wrenching changes are rare events, and they can't be repeated over and over.

Yet the market is demanding that we change over and over. To succeed, we need to have plastic surgery on a regular basis.

Change management doesn't know how to respond to this challenge. Change management is about minimizing the damage and maximizing the healing. Change management assumes that we can manage change. It assumes that change will go away and leave a new equilibrium in its wake.

Traditionally, change management is about explaining the reason for change, reassuring key employees that there's a better future in store, and then doing everything necessary to help the organization survive the change. By creating a sense of urgency combined with a promise of future safety, change managers work to cajole the organization into grudgingly accepting the changes.

Change management is dependent on emergencies. But change is no longer an emergency. Change is normal.

The Way to Build an Organization that Can Embrace Change Is to Redefine Change

If change equals death, then all the training sessions in the world won't create an environment of constant change. Yes, you can probably persuade people to pitch in on one or two change management efforts, but only by promising them that at the end of the process, there will be a new plateau, a period of "normalcy." We have a very strong genetic abhorrence of change, and triggering that change-avoidance reflex almost always leads to stress and a lack of success in getting anything changed.

In the organization I'm describing, though, change is the new normal and change management won't work. You can probably motivate someone to touch a snake once, but that's a different challenge from encouraging someone to become a snake handler.

Picasso evolved memetically dozens and dozens of times over his long career. He went through periods, pushed himself, learned, experimented and was a very different artist by the time he died. Yet throughout his entire career, he never changed his genes.

Did Picasso freeze in fear—like a deer caught in the headlights—every time he changed his style? It's unlikely. If Picasso had defined his move from genre to genre as "change," then his change-avoidance gene would have kicked in and he would have become a bricklayer or something safe.

It's easy to think of innovators like Picasso or entrepreneurs like Thomas Edison as risk-taking daredevils, but time and again, these people insist that they don't feel as if they are taking risks. Most innovators and entrepreneurs just redefine what risk means. Edison knew that if he made inventing stuff his regular job, he could happily move from invention to invention without getting stressed. Picasso took the same approach to his art.

The goal of the zooming process is to redefine change at work to be something that doesn't cause the change-avoidance gene to kick in with waves of fear and panic. If we can bypass that reflex, we can define "normal" as being an environment in which new memes appear on a regular basis.

Chapter 4

DO YOU ZOOM?

> Zooming is about stretching your limits without threatening your
> foundation. It's about handling new ideas, new opportunities and
> new challenges without triggering the change-avoidance reflex.

THIS IS NOTHING NEW TO YOU. You already bypass your
change-avoidance reflex every day: Whenever you buy a new
CD or read a new issue of *The New York Times,* you don't have to
contend with all of the emotions that we associate with "change."
You're zooming—doing the same thing as usual, only different. If
the stories in the paper were the same every day, or the songs on
the radio never changed, you'd hate that. They change, but it's
okay, because the change is something you signed up for.

Eating at a different Thai restaurant, trying a new airline—for
most of us, these things don't represent "change." This is the
stuff of exploration; it's the kind of thing that we're eager to do.
That's why the guidebook business is booming, and why adventure travel is a growth industry. These products and services offer
safe adventure—the chance to do the same thing as usual, only
different.

The goal is to turn these trivial sorts of zooming endeavors into efforts that have more impact. Instead of just zooming with *The New York Times,* you can learn to zoom with new business models or markets or production processes.

Zooming, you've probably noticed, is not the same thing as evolving. You need to zoom before you can evolve, because making frequent changes in the memes you embrace will allow you to discover which memes work for you. Zooming is about frequent meme changes, constant change, effortless change, but not necessarily change with an objective. That comes later.

There are all kinds of zoomers, and all kinds of categories in which you can learn to zoom. The late John Hammond was a world-class zoomer. Hammond was the guy at Columbia Records who discovered Billie Holiday, Count Basie, Aretha Franklin, Bob Dylan, and Bruce Springsteen. What made him a zoomer? He defined "the same thing as usual, only different" pretty broadly. He didn't spend his days trying to find folk singers, jazz singers, or crossover funky white singers. No, Hammond just looked for singers.

By choosing to zoom across such a large area, he was able to listen to anyone, any time, without triggering his genetic fear of real change. He didn't plague himself with rigid rules and standards; he just wanted to find something great. Hammond had broad "zoomwidth." I'm betting that if you had asked him whether finding all of those different kinds of singers meant that he had to "change" every day, he would have said no. He viewed each day not as a high-stress, change-filled event but as part of his zooming continuum.

Note that Hammond's catholic tastes in music didn't necessarily mean that he was always going to find a superstar. In his sixty-year career, he found many, many artists who failed to make an impact on the world. Zooming just allowed him to act like a fruit fly, frequently reshuffling his memes until he found a combination that worked.

Martha Stewart was able to translate her book-writing business into a $100-million media empire. It was all part of the same process. She couldn't have done this if she had defined her safe zone as one that included only books. By redefining what change meant, Stewart was able to focus her energy on building the business, rather than fighting her genetic urge to flee.

Compare her approach to the one taken by *Rolling Stone* magazine. Its editors were too entrenched in the magazine paradigm to see that they could have been MTV. The management of the magazine saw a move in that direction as a huge risk, a change not worth wrestling with. They weren't in enough pain to go through the change, so they focused on the magazine instead of zooming to something new.

Omaha Steaks realized that however they sold their steaks—by phone, by mail or on the Net—it was all the same thing, only different. By contrast, it took Lands' End years (and many meetings) to sell products online.

The Limited changes its merchandise at every single store at least once a month—whether it needs to or not. Does this mean that they get it right all the time? Absolutely not. In fact, they've had several years of bad luck. Regardless of the quality of the memes they try, they've figured out how to zoom. At Limited stores, introducing a new clothing style is easy: Managers don't have to go very far up in the organization to get approval.

Why is there so much pain in the business world? One reason is that most companies are now stretched beyond their zoomwidth. Everything that's new is seen as a threat; nothing is an opportunity. By increasing your zoomwidth—by learning how to zoom and then hiring people who want to zoom with you—your company can grow, adapt and maybe even transform itself.

Here's an important thing to remember about zooming: It's not something you do in response to a crisis. If a company faces disaster, it can't ask its people to start zooming. They will see the crisis and realize that they're being asked to change. And change is scary.

Ask most managers why they don't zoom and the answer will

be a combination of two factors. The first is that they will lose their jobs because their boss doesn't support the effort. And the second is that they are far too busy with their current issues and there's no time—if they allocated the time, their core business would fail and then everyone would lose their jobs.

This seems to make sense, but it's not true.

Adults in fear of change will tell you whatever they need to in order to avoid the real issue—that they're afraid. A quick trip to the local university exposes the flaw in most of the arguments that people present for being afraid to learn how to zoom. College professors with tenure are extremely unlikely to get fired. They have plenty of time to work on new projects. Thus, the two main reasons people give for not embracing change don't exist at a college.

You would think that this would lead to a hotbed of zooming, a campus filled with people eager to radically change many elements of their daily lives. Instead, you discover as much fear of change at a university as you'll find in most companies—it's not the measurable risks that people are trying to avoid when they resist change, it's their fear.

The difference between change management and zooming is simple. Change management is about a big change, an urgent

---

"You don't have to heal from zooming, any more than you need to heal from breathing."

---

change with a purpose. And it's a one-time event, followed by a period of healing.

Zooming, on the other hand, is about constant change, change for no particular reason, with no particular goal. And it's followed by ever more change, change in the service of evolution. You don't have to heal from zooming, any more than you need to heal from breathing.

Start Zooming Before the Crisis Comes

Isn't "zooming" just a lot of semantic maneuvering? Why waste time on a word or two? The zoomer's answer: Words are important. They give you a lens through which you can see why you (and your company) are finding it so hard to move as quickly as you'd like.

Every company zooms. Some zoom more than others. If your company zooms more than its competitors, you will be creating change and they will always be struggling to keep up. Increasing your zoomwidth is a challenge, but it builds an asset that pays off every day for your company.

The best time to start zooming is before your company is looking at a big, life-threatening change. Get into the habit of making frequent, small changes first. Then work your way up to bigger and bigger things.

No one freaks out if the color of the toothpick in his BLT sandwich changes. Over time, though, enough small changes can add up to a big change.

Here are five simple things that you can do to practice zooming.

1. For dinner tonight, eat a food that you've never tasted. Then try another one tomorrow night.

2. On your way to work tomorrow, listen to a CD from a musical genre that you hate or that's new to you.

3. Every week, read a magazine that you've never read before.

4. Once a week, meet with someone from outside your area of expertise. Go to a trade show on a topic in which you have no interest whatsoever.

5. Change the layout of your office.

Sounds stupid, doesn't it? Like a bad self-improvement book. But if you can master these five steps, you're much more likely to have the confidence to invent five new steps. Gradually, you can increase the circles of change that you can happily accept. Then you'll discover that the art of zooming makes it easier for you to view everything as an opportunity. In other words, you'll find that it's easier to sign Bob Dylan when you thought you were looking for Count Basie.

What About the Creative Corporation?

Tom Peters captured our imagination a decade ago with his insistence that we turn work into a "crazy, zany" place that was fun, imaginative and new. He insisted that we appoint a Vicar of Vitality and turn up the volume at work. Our companies are stuck, he pointed out, and if we don't figure out how to lighten up, loosen up and get a little crazy, we're dead.

I took his words to heart. In any given environment, I was the wackiest, the weirdest, the one most willing to push the envelope (except for one employee I had who wore purple slippers to work, but that's a different story). Two things about this astonished me:

- Being weird worked wonders. Pushing the envelope of an organization's zoomwidth always seemed to work.

- Most people have *a lot* of trouble taking initiative and taking chances. It stresses them out.

Being weird doesn't work, though.
Your coworkers will push back. They'll view "outlandish" behavior as annoying or obnoxious. The obstacle to widespread acceptance of the Peters prescription is that it threatens the status quo.

The problem is simple: aggressively testing new hypotheses and venturing into new areas may be profitable, but we're genetically programmed to flee from activities like that. Tom Peters has it exactly right—except that most people can't pull it off. It can't be done.

Work is a place for measurement and stability and safety and bringing food home for our genes. Even in the middle of the Internet revolution, the most successful companies were, at some level,

---

"The obstacle to widespread acceptance of the Peters prescription is that it threatens the status quo."

---

the most boring. It takes more than purple furniture and a capital letter in the middle of your company name to be weird.

It's too hard to institutionalize weirdness. Too difficult to measure insight and creativity and out-of-the-box thinking. Too much to ask to have people take initiative in different ways in different circumstances. It would be great if everyone would, but they don't and they won't.

The magic of zooming is that it allows the people you work with to train themselves to grow *incrementally,* one different-colored toothpick at a time. Now we can use the same incremental improvement techniques we use in a factory to improve our ability to learn new things. That's why zooming is actually the fastest way to get to where Tom is going—it bypasses the fear and the speed bumps of the more direct journey. Now, everyone is weird. Which means, of course, that no one is weird.

Zoom First and Ask Questions Later

Companies that are already zooming don't have much trouble evolving. Once it's easy for changes to ripple through an organization without leaving a wake of angry, confused and stunned employees, those ripples start to take the company to new places—good places—quite quickly.

The challenge isn't in learning how to evolve. It's in zooming.

The first thing organizations that don't zoom ask about a proposed change is, "Can you guarantee it will work?" They want an assurance that whatever change you're about to put them through is better than what they've already got.

There's no shortage of good ideas out there. Even when an entrenched company's competitors are gaining market share and maximizing profits, it's easy to find naysayers who insist that there isn't enough proof to make the entire organization go through a change—they're sure the threat is no threat at all.

A vivid example is the way nonprofits have reacted to the Internet. A few have demonstrated how well they can use the medium for fundraising, for coordinating volunteers and for grant writing. Yet most nonprofits are still on the fence, waiting for the new medium to prove itself. While they sit and wait for the proof that will never be enough, competitors (other charities asking for donations, for volunteers, for grants) step in to fill the gap.

Big, established nonprofits rarely learn to zoom. They're not rewarded for it, they're not organized for it and they don't hire for it. As a result, they get stuck.

Inertia keeps an object at rest from moving. Once an object starts moving, though, momentum keeps it moving.

The same inertia works at a company. Getting a company into motion is far more difficult than keeping it there. Rather than accepting a cycle in which almost all of our time is spent living with the pain of initiating and selling change, companies need to abandon the cycle and embrace the idea of changing all the time. Some of your coworkers will be unable to live with that and they'll leave. That will only lead to a company that changes faster still. And if you attract new employees who embrace this new dynamic, you're on your way to runaway.

> "Getting a company into motion is far more difficult than keeping it there."

Does runaway last forever? Of course not. Companies get too big, they slow down, markets change in ever more unexpected ways. Even Microsoft won't grow forever. But this is a great bridge to cross when you get to it. Most of us never even get close.

Comparing Zooming to Re-engineering

Most companies that re-engineered did so in order to make the "machine" more efficient. This usually meant laying off people. According to CSC Index, a consulting firm heavily involved in re-engineering, more than 70 percent of the employees involved in these efforts assumed that their purpose was to lead to layoffs.

Zooming is almost diametrically opposed to this position. A zooming organization isn't worried about making today's machine work better. It's worried about being flexible enough to put its assets to work building tomorrow's machine. The management of a zooming company must communicate to the people who work there that the goal isn't to get smaller—it's to get more flexible. Flexible companies make better use of their assets, and the first asset they maximize is their people.

You can't shrink your way to greatness.

Of course, not everyone is guaranteed a job. Some folks will insist on sitting still, or being told what to do. If they can't change to a new role, then they're holding the company back. But just about everyone in an organization can zoom if they choose to. Zooming leads to the launch of runaway successes, which leads to better hiring, which leads to even faster zooming and the continu-

---

"You can't shrink your way to greatness."

---

ation of the runaway cycle. While it's easy to fear any process of change, the process of zooming is far more optimistic than the shrink-to-productivity approach of re-engineering.

Avoid the Dragon, Don't Slay It

Jeanie Daniel Duck is a partner at the Boston Consulting Group, and her new book *The Change Monster* is all about why companies have so much trouble implementing change. She outlines a multi-step process that every company goes through as it moves from here to there.

It starts, she says, with stagnation. This leads to enough pain that senior management makes a decision. Smart companies then prepare for change, begin to implement it and, if they're lucky, survive the "conflicts, clashes and failures," that ensue. They persevere through the crisis and either abandon the change effort or have it come to fruition.

"Just abandon the change monster. Skip the plateaus and embrace the idea of an always-changing entity where change is not threatening, just part of the job."

This is the way it's always been. We don't change until we have to, we survive the change and then everything goes back to normal.

But now things *won't* go back to normal. That used to be true.

The plateaus were long enough that they felt like calm places where we could avoid change for a while. But now, change is happening faster and faster and it comes with overhead: Initiating and processing change is difficult and expensive.

Just abandon the change monster. Skip the plateaus and embrace the idea of an always-changing entity where change is not threatening, just part of the job.

Which Sort of Pain Are You Going to Feel?

The hundreds of years of asset-based, command-and-control commerce have affected all of us. From single employees to vast corporations, most people approach the world using the same paradigm: Go to school. Get a degree. Take one job, or two or three. By then, you've labeled yourself. You're a project manager or a cashier or an accountant. Over time, you move up the ladder, perfecting your skills, increasing the value of your personal asset, getting very specific in the things you know how to do. You have a winning strategy and you're sticking with it. The goal is for the world to stay reasonably stable until you've got enough money to retire.

You go to work for a company. The company values its physical assets highly, its intellectual assets almost as highly, its people not highly enough. The company has a winning strategy and the goal

---

"The alternative is to reorganize for change, go through the pain and suffering of just one more change, and then be done with it."

---

of everyone at the company is to get enough out of the winning strategy that by the time the company goes bankrupt (as all companies eventually do) we'll all be gone.

At every step, as our assets get more valuable, we become more attached to the winning strategy that makes those assets valuable.

And as we get more hooked on the winning strategy, we become far less likely to acknowledge that it might not be the best strategy any longer. That means that change in the competitive landscape is painful. Layoffs hurt. New technology is a threat. New competitors and a changed landscape are things to be feared.

For now, most of us have chosen to live with this fear. It's long-lasting, certain and chronic. There's an alternative, though. The alternative is to reorganize for change, go through the pain and suffering of just one more change, and then be done with it.

If your new winning strategy is that nothing is certain, that change is not only inevitable but welcome, then you won't be disappointed. Imagine that.

Chapter 5

YOUR COMPANY HAS mDNA

Organizations can put the proven tactics of evolution to use by embracing change, not fighting it. By incorporating adopting successful new memes into a company's mDNA, organizations can defeat their slower competitors.

The Vocabulary of Genes and Memes in Nature and at Work

Words like zoom and meme and mDNA and phrases like **Red Queen** and **Muller's Ratchet** are not normally heard in corporate America. Which is exactly why you need to teach them to the people you work with. Without the words to talk about a new way of thinking, we'll surely revert to the old way of thinking. Yes, you can look at this new way of doing business through an old lens, but that means you'll be trying to build your understanding around the old memes instead of creating a new way of doing business.

Full disclosure: This is not a genomics textbook, so I've taken liberties with many of these definitions. Please don't bring them with you when you take your final exam in Evolution 101.

Nature	Business
Gene—the basic building block of an organism; the functional unit of heredity	**Meme**—the basic building block of an organization's winning strategy and its tactics; the functional unit of idea transference

Nature	Business
DNA—the molecule that carries the genetic code; commonly used by laymen to describe the sum of all the genes and the protein effects of those genes as well	**mDNA**—the sum of all the memes, people and assets in an organization
Genomics—the study of genes and their function	**Zoometry**—the study (and influence) of mDNA
Length of generation—contributes to how fast or slowly a species adapts through genetic evolution	**Periodicity**—affects how fast or slowly a company adapts through memetic evolution
Extinct—species that didn't evolve and lost their ecological niche to a more fit organism	**Stuck winning strategy**—an organization's tendency to reject improved memes (which always leads to losing a market niche, and ultimately, bankruptcy, a form of extinction)
Sexual selection—choosing mates in a way that affect the traits of future offspring in the species	**Sexual selection**—hiring and firing of employees and customers in a way that affects the future of the organization
Natural selection—only fit animals live long enough to reproduce	**Natural selection**—only companies with winning strategies are able to hire people, sell products and raise money
Gene pool—the variations available to a species through random mating	**Meme pool**—the business variations available to a company as it varies its winning strategy
Fitness—lifetime reproductive success of an individual organism	**Fitness**—success of a corporation from a particular winning strategy (growth could be measured in profits, employees hired, memes spread)
Signaling device—cues that communicate one organism's fitness to a potential mate or competitor	**Signaling device**—cues that communicate a company's fitness to a potential employee, competitor or customer

Nature	Business
Ecological niche—space in the ecosystem where an organism can thrive	**Business niche**—space in the competitive environment where a company can thrive
Mutation—error in the transmission of genetic information during reproduction	**Mutation**—abrupt change (accidental or intentional) in a meme that is part of a company's winning strategy
The Red Queen—competitive change in the ecosystem created by the responses to one species's evolution, creating a cycle of coevolution	**The Red Queen**—competitive change in the marketplace created by the responses to one company's evolution, creating a cycle of coevolution
Muller's Ratchet—continual decrease in fitness of an asexual species due to accumulation of mutations	**Muller's Ratchet**—continual decrease in fitness of an organization due to the stagnation that comes from hiring only people who agree with you and working only for clients who don't push
Disposable Soma Theory—species doesn't benefit from evolving to extend life of an organism beyond a certain point	**Disposable Soma Theory**—competitive advantage due to a company's longevity decreases if it leads to a stuck winning strategy
Runaway—rapid evolution that comes when a positive feedback loops exists between sexual selection and inheritance	**Runaway**—rapid evolution that occurs when a company is able to find new customers and new employees that reinforce its winning strategy of zooming and evolving

The Power of the Metaphor

The tactics that we need to implement to deal with change are not really obvious or natural or easy to adopt. Without a guiding metaphor, it's unlikely that you'd even experiment with what I'm proposing. But if the metaphor fits, if you can find a way to harness the power of one of nature's best inventions, it's going to be far easier to sell this effective new approach to your colleagues and investors. So, with the caveats I'll introduce in a little bit, here's the metaphor:

If we define DNA as being the genes and proteins and genetic code that, when combined, define an organism and determine much of that organism's development, then the organism you call your company has DNA. (I call it mDNA because the analogy isn't perfect and I want to distinguish memes from genes.)

Your mDNA is made up of the rules, processes, policies, market position and people in a company.

Without this mDNA, your company would forget, from day to day, what it was, what it did and how it did it. The factories you own, the policies you follow, the brands you market today—they all determine how you're going to do business tomorrow.

Every day, your body replaces missing skin cells, grows new hair and processes insulin. It couldn't do this reliably or with any consistency unless your DNA told it how.

Similarly, when you go into work tomorrow, the vast majority

"The factories you own, the policies you follow, the brands you market today—they all determine how you're going to do business tomorrow."

---

of your tasks for the day are already set for you. You don't start with a blank slate, because of your company's mDNA.

Your mDNA determines whom you're going to hire next. It allows employees to make decisions without running each issue past the CEO. Your mDNA includes instructions on everything from pricing to service to which companies to acquire next. It may not be stored in an easily readable string like human DNA, but it's there nonetheless.

Unlike human DNA, your mDNA can mutate as often as your

business wants it to. The mDNA must change before the organization can change. Trying to change a business (and the people who work there) without mutating the mDNA is impossible.

Why Evolution Works

Evolution among animals works for two reasons:

1. There are lots of animals

2. They've got plenty of time

With literally billions of fruit flies reproducing every day, for example, it's pretty likely that sooner or later a few of them are going to get lucky and produce a better fruit fly. Add to this the fact that the billions of fruit flies have millions of years to get their act together. Over the millennia, they produce offspring that are smarter, faster, more resilient, stronger . . . somehow more adapted for the competitive environment in which they live. Natural selection ensures that the most fit fruit flies are likeliest to reproduce.

As Jostein Gaarder, the author of *Sophie's World*, said, "Evolution is a lottery where we only see the winning tickets."

At the same time, female fruit flies are picky about which males they choose. With generation after generation absorbing the results of the previous generation's sexual selection, the engine of evolution guarantees that the gene pool is always evolving and that the fruit flies are always in a great position to deal with competition and change in their environment.

Finally, remember that it only takes a week or so for a generation of fruit flies to go from newborn to fertile. This rapid evolutionary cycle further increases their adaptability.

Sounds a little like the market your company competes in,

doesn't it? There are always new companies willing to try anything to get a foothold, and old competitors who periodically launch a new product or technology. If you're just one fruit fly (company) competing against millions of others, it's inevitable someone else is going to evolve something useful.

"If you want to teach a squirrel to swim, you can yell and scream and offer it little squirrel treats. Or you could realize that a squirrel doesn't have the DNA to swim and instead work to breed a swimming squirrel. It's a lot less painful—for you and for the squirrel."

Unlike the fruit flies, though, that are unconscious and stuck with the genes they're born with, your company can borrow a successful meme as soon as you discover it. (Except that most companies rarely do.)

- What would happen if instead of fighting any change to the memes that make up its mDNA, a company made it easy to change its mDNA? This flexible, plastic mDNA would be more open to mutating when the competitive environment demanded it.

- Add to this a healthy dose of sexual selection. Companies could realize that attracting new mDNA in the form of new hires that were more fit (and conversely, getting rid of bad mDNA in the form of aggressive firing) would dramatically and permanently improve the company's meme pool.

- And finally, consider the impact of shortening the length of a generation. Instead of reorganizing every ten years or getting a new CEO every twenty years or adopting new policies every three, a company could see itself as an always-reproducing organism. By shortening generations an order of magnitude or more, the company evolves that much faster.

If you want to teach a squirrel to swim, you can yell and scream and offer it little squirrel treats. Or you could realize that a squirrel doesn't have the DNA to swim and instead work to breed a swimming squirrel. It's a lot less painful—for you and for the squirrel.

Companies Evolve

You work in a swamp. Or a rain forest. Depends on your point of view.

Either way, it's an environment that's teeming with life. The marketplace is incredibly fertile, spawning new life (businesses) and new variations all the time. A jungle, a swamp, a rain forest—they're all teeming with life, reeking with fecundity, and as a result, the site of much evolution. Just like your company.

If your business is successful, you're constantly fighting off new competitors and new competitive threats. As time goes by, your company changes in response to this competition.

If you're stressed at work, if your company is struggling with change, it's because management is trying to change the behavior of employees without changing the company's memes first.

Some species are more adaptive than others. Remember the fruit fly and the platypus? An adaptive species is defined as one that is organized to change its DNA whenever the environment demands it. This is likely to occur in species with a short generational cycle (lots of babies, very often) or in species with genes that mutate productively, or those that have useful sexual selection. Regardless of how it happens, adaptive species outperform those that aren't.

All sorts of environmental factors contribute to how your company evolves. If you've got a stereo store in Buffalo, New York, the competition from the truly amazing Stereo Advantage store across town forces you to discover ways to cut costs and win on price without sacrificing service. If your stereo store is competing in Palo Alto, California, on the other hand, you're discovering through trial and error that comfy couches and snooty salespeople are the secret to your success.

Saturn, the legendary small-car division of General Motors, evolved in deliberate isolation. It's definitely not Oldsmobile. While every other GM brand is very much part of the mothership, Saturn set out to follow its own course. They built their factories and offices in Tennessee, not Michigan. They brought in management and employees who could build a relationship of mutual respect, as opposed to repeating the normally antagonistic relationship between management and labor that all other American car plants are built around. The Saturn plant has about three basic job classifications, while a typical GM plant has seventy or more. The Saturn plant has three or four levels of hierarchy while the typical GM plant has six or more.

Saturn has different job titles, pay scales, work rules, corporate culture, parking lot hierarchy, product lines, quality expectations and advertising. Except for the fact that they also make cars, it's hard to find many similarities between GM and the division they spawned.

Part of the reason that Saturn evolved so quickly was that the entire staff walked in with no status quo to defend. According to one former Saturn employee, "You had to like risk, because as a new employee, they couldn't make any assurances about your job security. . . . You had to be willing to go into a new unit that potentially in three months would disappear."

Over the years, Saturn has grown farther and farther apart from GM. While it was intended to be a laboratory for best-of-breed thinking that could come back to improve GM, the division instead acts almost like a competitor. GM management appears to go out of its way not to interact with Saturn—it's as though the two companies, which started as one organism, have evolved to become two different species.

When Anna Kretz, the hourly employee quoted earlier, was asked how much of Saturn's learning she was able to bring back with her when she transferred to a new job somewhere else at General Motors, she had a startling, one-word answer, "Nothing." The techniques and information couldn't transfer any more than a moose can fertilize a donkey.

Or consider the story of Cynthia Trudell, who was installed by GM as chairwoman and president of Saturn in 1999. After only two years as a GM insider (and Saturn outsider) she threw in the towel and left the company to run a boat-building operation. Saturn now has its own mDNA, and other organizations and employees with a different view of the world can't mate with it.

GM couldn't zoom, so they created a division that could. That division evolved, quite naturally, without GM there keeping it from evolving. The end result, though, wasn't what GM hoped for. They created a new species, and reintegrating the companies has proved far more difficult than GM expected.

Evolution from the Ground Up

The giant system we call "business" is really many smaller systems, all entwined.

Change starts with you, the employee. You work in a department, or a group. That group makes up a division, which constitutes a company. The company is part of a system that might be called an industry sector or vertical market. And ultimately, your company, all your competitors and all the other industry sectors out there complete the picture.

At each step along the way, there's a memetic code and competition and mDNA and evolution. When a division starts racking up more sales, it gets more employees, becomes more influential within the company, advances the careers of the people who work there and changes the fabric of the parent company (at the same time it disturbs the competitive balance of its market). Enron, for example, evolved from pumping natural gas to selling data and creating markets. The mDNA of the company has shifted radically over the last ten years as one business has become far more successful.

While most executives like to start from the top and work their way down an organization, evolution doesn't think that way. Instead, it's the individual organism that drives the process. If a species of animal starts dominating an ecosystem, it didn't happen because of a centralized decision. It happened because a few animals were more fit than their competition, and they passed that fitness on to their offspring.

Your résumé combined with the people you know and your personal brand and reputation and the rules you follow constitute the mDNA you bring to work every day. You're the key element in your organization's evolution, since it is you and your coworkers that determine which paths the company takes.

If you and your colleagues zoom, then you'll evolve faster, become more fit and win more often. This example can then spread through the organization.

Moving one step up the ladder, your company consists of the mDNA and winning strategies of all its employees, working together, separately or at odds with one another. Just as your liver

---

"If you and your colleagues zoom, then you'll evolve faster, become more fit and win more often."

---

isn't always concerned with how your left kneecap feels, it's not unusual for various segments of a company to be at war with each other, each working to defeat the other in competition for resources.

A step higher, entire markets evolve as well. A new technology can affect an industry, and the entire industry can respond by changing its mDNA. The behavior of the pharmaceutical industry in Africa as it adjusted prices for AIDS medication is a fine example of a market changing its mDNA. Every pharmaceutical company is now adjusting its actions to deal with the new market realities of governments and NGOs becoming involved in pharmaceutical pricing.

So you've got your personal business mDNA, interacting in a competitive space with others who would like your job. You evolve to get better and better jobs and to beat that competition.

Your coworkers join with you to create an organization that can win more than its fair share of resources within your company. If you succeed, you hire more people, do cooler projects and improve your personal mDNA as well.

Meanwhile, your company is competing with other companies and evolving to become more fit in the battle you face not just with entrenched competitors, but with the companies that might enter your field.

And on and on. Evolution of complex systems like these involves far too many elements for the harried middle manager to process on a whiteboard.

But it's not chaos.

If you look at genetic evolution the wrong way, it seems like nothing but noise. Billions of organisms with no one in charge, all reproducing as fast as they can and competing for one ecological niche or another.

But at the most extreme close-up, evolution makes perfect sense. Two organisms compete and the one that wins passes on its genes. And at the least extreme close-up, it makes sense again. Over the course of millions of years, this apparently senseless turbulence has produced the human eye and the elk and the skunk and *Apollo 11*. It's only in those in-between views that evolution appears unorganized and teetering on the edge of disaster.

The same is true of the evolving organization. If the "rules" are established properly, the work that goes on at the micro level will make perfect sense. The decisions that are made, the trade-offs that occur, will all be rational and testable. And in the largest sense, the organization will thrive and enter and re-enter runaway as it furthers its lead on its competitors.

It's only in the middle, at the desk of the harried middle manager who desires control and has none, that it appears to be a total disaster. And so far, most corporate change-management efforts have focused on the middle, because that's where bulk meets power. It's no wonder that few organizations have embraced the idea of zooming. The people who need to do the embracing have to change the most.

The Red Queen Goes to Work

In nature, evolution is everywhere. Many parasites evolve inside other organisms. Ecosystems evolve in response to those organisms, and competitors evolve in response to all of those factors. There are processes within (and next to) other processes. The same is true in business.

In *Through the Looking-Glass*, Lewis Carroll wrote about the Red Queen, caught on a chessboard in which every move changed the make-up of the entire board. Carroll's name for a character in an ever-changing competitive environment has been appropriated by evolutionary biologists to describe the coevolution that goes on between species and their competitors and parasites. The minute one species gets a head start, the landscape changes again, forcing other species to respond.

Your company is made up of employees. Each employee is evolving his or her own career mDNA. Some evolve quite quickly, learning new skills, finding other jobs within the company or leaving when the opportunities elsewhere are better. Divisions within your company evolve, usually in response to strong external competition or talented internal leadership. Individuals and divisions together drive the evolution of the entire organization.

While your organization is evolving, so is the competition. So are the financial markets, the technology base, the economy. All of these factors are changing every day, and the impact of these external forces is felt in your company as well.

Many of the companies that suffered from dot-com meltdown did so because the strategy they built their company on was completely dependent on fixed assumptions about the environment. These companies assumed that the financial markets would be stable, or that future financing would come on precisely the same terms as past financing, or that their customers would always be

---

"While your organization is evolving, so is the competition. So are the financial markets, the technology base, the economy. All of these factors are changing every day, and the impact of these external forces is felt in your company as well."

---

as euphoric as they once were. They were nailed when the assumptions proved untrue.

Or consider the plight facing Sony as they get ready to launch a new video game system. The PlayStation was designed to compete with products from Sega and Nintendo, among others. The designers were also aware of the growing use of personal computers to play video games, and they knew that Microsoft was readying its own game player.

If the playing field were static, it would be reasonable for Sony to have mapped out a fixed strategy for the development and launch of the system. But the entire marketplace they face is in flux.

Internally, Sony has to work to attract the world's best engineers (from competitors) and keep the ones they already have. Of course, the folks who are seemingly the most qualified to work at a certain level on this project are probably interested in working at a higher level, so they can continue evolving their careers. That means Sony has to take a chance and give the best people they can find a shot at a task they've not yet mastered.

Externally, Sony is fighting against Moore's Law, which means that by the time their system is ready, new computer chips coming onto the market will be at least twice as fast as they were the day Sony started work on the project. They must also be prepared for unknown competitors, working in secret, readying their own machines.

The Sony player may be dependent on chips made by other companies, and unknown to Sony, the price and availability of those chips is about to become another source of chaos. Sony ended up shipping half as many PlayStations as they had orders for last Christmas, entirely because of a chip shortage.

Finally, Sony must face the fact that after the product is launched, the Red Queen will return. Sony's entry will change the market again, raising the bar for everyone else and making it that much harder for Sony to be the state of the art for long.

Managing during turbulent times becomes far more complex because of the Russian nesting dolls of evolution within evolution.

"You can't manage change. Change manages you."

If all you had to do was manage one highly visible changing system, it would probably be worth attempting. But the systems are far more complex than that. And so your management posture is far more important than the actual data you interact with every day. Seeing the systems within the systems and respecting them prepares you for the chaos to come.

You can't manage change. Change manages you.

One Good Reason That CEOs Reject Evolution as an Alternative—and Why They're Wrong

Earlier, I wrote about how evolution can lead to a dead end. A species (like T. Rex) can evolve in response to competitive conditions, only to discover itself way out on a limb when conditions change.

CEOs understand that the market isn't always right. In fact, it's frequently wrong. Look no farther than the dot-com meltdown to see an example of irrational exuberance that led many companies to evolve in precisely the wrong direction—only to fail a few years later.

The CEO argues that evolution works best in hindsight. We can see what *did* work, and then explain the presence of various species based on their continued existence. Fur is a great adaptation, the evolutionary biologists argue, because if it weren't, there wouldn't be furry animals! We rarely see what mutations *didn't* work, so we're not often called upon to explain why there are no purple squirrels or goldfish the size of moose.

Businesses, on the other hand, need to look forward, not back. It doesn't make us any money if we successfully understand why

---

"So the smart CEO will tell you that her job is to be smarter than evolution. Her job is to see beyond today's hot trend and embrace the future instead."

---

strategy A was better than strategy B. What we need to do is predict which strategy is going to work in the future.

So the smart CEO will tell you that her job is to be smarter than evolution. Her job is to see beyond today's hot trend and embrace the future instead.

Except that the job of the CEO is not to be right. That's impossible. No company has consistently been smarter than the marketplace. (GE under the mighty Jack Welch included. His astonishing track record has made him the patron saint of many business magazines. Yet the Honeywell debacle—his swan song—proves my point.) The job of the CEO is to organize the company to jump on board a strategy that's winning *for now* and, at the same time, to

---

"... the job of the CEO is not to be right. That's impossible. No company has consistently been smarter than the marketplace."

---

organize the company to evolve often enough to find the next strategy before today's strategy disappears.

Pets.com had a smart strategy when it was founded. They raised plenty of money and had no trouble finding smart employees. So what went wrong?

They fell in love with their strategy and organized around one idea, instead of building a company resilient enough to respond to the environment. When the first strategy fell apart (when it became clear that it would take years to grow big enough to be profitable) they were unable to move their smart people and their remaining piles of money to a new strategy. So they slowly faded to bankruptcy instead.

While we'd like to believe that we're smarter than the market, we're not. The track record of every entertainment, manufacturing and services company CEO demonstrates that while markets morph and change around us, no one has a perfect track record in determining what's going to happen next. In fact, most people do far worse than average in predicting the future. (Sound impossible? Read the next paragraph.)

If we look at one easily measured market—the stock market—we find that over the last twenty years, less than 9 percent of all mutual funds have outperformed the S&P 500, which is nothing but an automatic market basket of five hundred stocks. Ninety-one percent of the funds do worse than average, yet each and every one of these mutual fund managers was hired and paid to beat the index.

With a 91 percent failure rate on just a twenty-year time horizon, why should we expect that our track record is going to be any different?

Evolution works because the tireless efforts of trillions of entities will always defeat central planning. That's little solace for the organism that evolves only to discover that it's ill-equipped for the environment. You don't care that sooner or later, evolution will figure it out. You want *your* product, *your* company, *your* investment to succeed. As your bets get bigger and the stakes get higher, the temptation to abandon evolution and stick with watching all those eggs in that basket is nearly overwhelming. But evolution is our single most reliable and effective strategy for dealing with change. The challenge for management, then, is to figure out how to put this strategy to work.

There's another way to look at it: No one had a meeting and decided that this somewhat chaotic way of creating the future was the best way. It's certainly wasteful in the short run and even painful. That doesn't matter. What matters is the reality that this is the way it works. You don't have to agree with it or like it, it just is.

As long as there are entrepreneurs willing to take risks, sources of capital willing to fund them and employees willing to give it a try, there will always be chaos in the markets. And in today's networked world, the chaos is getting worse. Your choice is to respond to it, by beating the turbulence at its own game, or to react to it, by getting frantic when it's too late to make any difference.

CEOs Enjoy Picking Lottery Numbers

Why are managers predisposed to reject evolution as a winning business strategy? Every manager has a choice: She can build an organization that responds to change by evolving, or she can design a company that relies on decrees from top management about strategy and tactics. So why do almost all managers choose the latter?

Western capitalism is based on the idea of control, particularly control by the boss. Signing up for a fast-track job at a big company means years of doing what you're told, followed by decades of telling other people what to do. We rationalize this behavior because it seems to work . . . every ship has a captain, after all, because otherwise we'd never get anywhere.

Unfortunately, people frequently confuse control with impact. Consider a scientific study about control that was done with lottery tickets. Two groups were given free lotto tickets. The first group was given tickets with the number already chosen for them. The second group got to pick their lotto number.

Just hours before the lotto drawing was supposed to take place, the researchers asked the subjects to sell them back their tickets. The average price demanded by the folks with predetermined lotto tickets was two dollars. The average price for the tickets of the people that had control over their number, however, was eight dollars.

Obviously, choosing their own numbers did nothing at all to increase the odds that they were going to win the lottery. Yet apparently rational people placed a 400 percent higher value on those tickets. Why? Because they enjoyed feeling as though they were in control and transferred that feeling into the irrational belief that it would increase their odds of winning.

CEOs do the same thing with their spreadsheets and analyst reports and the macho certainty that their vision of the future is correct.

Of course, it's not just CEOs. In my work with Flatiron Partners, a leading New York venture capital firm, I've heard hundreds of entrepreneurs make pitches for their fledgling companies. These businesspeople know that if they make a persuasive presentation, they can walk out with millions of dollars of investment capital, along with the imprimatur and support of a top VC firm. So the stakes are high.

In not one of these presentations has the entrepreneur walked in and said, "We've got really smart people, an excellent attitude and an organization that's designed to evolve and change. We're not sure what the future brings, but we are sure that we've got the fast feedback loops and bias to evolve that we'll need to stay ahead of the competition."

I actually tried this when I was running my start-up company, but after twenty unsuccessful financing pitches I learned to keep my mouth shut and pretend that I knew exactly where the future lay.

In the middle of these traditional fundraising pitches, in which the management team has described the future in detail, I'm usually ready to burst. All I want to say is, "Okay, but what if you're wrong? What if the software isn't done on time or there is a competitor or the stock market tanks or your key salesperson quits to be a full-time dad or there's a fire in your R&D facility or . . ."

Dealing with the unexpected is usually a footnote. It's an afterthought on page forty-four of the business plan, "Our robust solution set is flexible enough to deal with other situations as well."

Hey. Given that 100 percent of the business plans for start-ups, and 100 percent of the strategic plans for big companies and 100 percent of the back-of-the-envelope hunches for midsized companies are wrong, perhaps the allocation of time and energy spent is wrong as well.

I'll admit that the benefit of creating a scenario in detail cannot be underestimated. Understanding how your business will thrive given one particular set of facts is critical if you are to have any hope of building a real company, or of making reasonable business-building investments. But relying on that analysis as the truth, depending on that analysis for success—that's crazy. Too often, companies organize themselves around one and only one

---

"Too often, companies organize themselves around one and only one winning strategy and then rely on plan P when the external factors don't pan out. Alas, plan P is to panic."

---

winning strategy and then rely on plan P when the external factors don't pan out. Alas, plan P is to panic.

For some reason, this set of facts is currently acceptable to employees and investors. Just take a look at the list of excuses that CEOs manage to come up with to deal with Wall Street when they have to report bad news. "Markets didn't mature as expected . . . currency fluctuations in Asia . . . uncertainties in technology adoption . . . unavoidable delays due to safety concerns . . . unforeseen bad weather conditions . . ." The only surprising thing about these surprises is that they shouldn't have been surprises. The weather is always different from what we expect. Currencies always fluctuate.

Yet investors accept these excuses. We continue to fool ourselves into believing that there is a chance (even a small chance) that everything will go according to plan. It won't, and it doesn't.

You'll note that I wrote "currently acceptable." As more companies demonstrate that embracing uncertainty is a viable business strategy, our patience with those that don't will evaporate.

Just because you picked the numbers on the lotto card doesn't mean that you're more likely to win the lottery.

I'm not proposing that chaos should reign at your company. Far from it. Chaos shouldn't reign, but it should have a much larger say in the way things are run. Management still has the vitally important job of deciding where to allocate resources. The boss still has to determine which fields are worth pursuing, which projects should be canceled, which processes can no longer be profitably improved. But there needs to be far more chaos and far less control.

Evolution at Wal-Mart

A few years ago, I flew to Bentonville, Arkansas, at the invitation of Wal-Mart's management. Bentonville is an unlikely site for the headquarters of the world's largest retailer, but there it is, an unattractive dark-brown aluminum shed in the middle of a huge field.

It's not fancy, but it works. Wal-Mart did $17 billion in sales last year. They had huge profits and their growth shows no sign of slowing. How did they do it?

The answer was right there on the wall of the lobby. A tiny black-and-white picture shows a rundown hardware store, circa 1962. This is the first Wal-Mart. Sam Walton did not get his start by building a one-hundred-thousand-square-foot store that sold guns, bananas and overalls. Nope. He opened a modest (actually, it was pretty tiny) hardware store in his hometown.

So what separated Sam Walton from the thousands of other people who opened little hardware stores in overlooked towns all over the country? One principle. Sam was obsessed with testing, measuring and implementing. *He organized to evolve.*

Every day (sometimes every hour) Sam would try something new. He'd gather every bit of data he could about the test and then test something else.

By testing and measuring, Sam discovered a pricing strategy

that still works. By testing and measuring, Sam discovered a store location strategy that still works. Wal-Mart now has a database with more than a billion items of information in it. They've used it, for example, to discover that people who buy bananas frequently buy milk. By putting a display of high-profit bananas near the milk, they dramatically increased banana sales (and profit).

For twenty years, Sam Walton tested and measured (and then implemented) every principle he could. He built open systems that let his suppliers do the same thing. More than 98 percent of the items in a Wal-Mart never see the inside of a Wal-Mart warehouse. They go straight from the manufacturer to the store. And manufacturers who want to do business with Wal-Mart but don't learn to use (and profit from) the Wal-Mart system don't last very long.

During the twenty formative years of Wal-Mart's evolution, Kmart was steadfastly resisting change at every turn. They stuck with their strategy and worked as hard as possible to milk the maximum benefit from their position as a leading retailer in the most profitable country in the world.

The people who work at Wal-Mart don't feel as if they change every day. They don't panic. Their strategy is surprisingly fixed:

They test and measure and implement what they learn. And they do it with large stores in small towns. Wal-Mart doesn't

---

"For twenty years, Sam Walton tested and measured (and then implemented) every principle he could."

---

spend any time at all testing the prospect of getting into the car-manufacturing business or experimenting with producing movies. The boundaries of their strategy are carved in stone, but within those boundaries they test like crazy.

Wal-Mart changes its mDNA every day. They use the feedback

loops they'd established to learn from what worked. They have evolved into a store very different from that first store in Rogers, Arkansas.

Kmart stayed still.

That's why, twenty years later, Wal-Mart, not Kmart, is number one.

Natural Selection and Artificial Selection

Evolution in the wild works, in large measure, due to natural selection. Survival of the fittest—the losers die. An animal is fit when it can survive and defeat less fit organisms in a search for food and mates. But that's not how Darwin came to prove his most important point. He used artificial selection instead. Artificial selection gave us the dachshund, the featherless chicken and the rose. Human beings can interfere in the workings of natural selection on domesticated plants and animals and breed species to turn out the way we choose.

If we encourage those organisms we like to reproduce (and discard those we don't like), it doesn't take very long to create a completely different breed of a species. Dog breeders do it all the time. **Artificial selection** is swift and powerful. Your company can benefit from the same technique.

What if companies weren't so quick to hire the very first qualified person to walk in the door? And what if we were very quick to fire people who failed to create and spread the memes we desired? Rather than treating jobs as cogs in a well-tuned machine, management could treat building an organization as an opportunity to perform artificial selection. It's not the heritage of corporate America to act this way, but it's an essential step in building a company that evolves.

We can redefine "qualified" to include all the zooming characteristics that are vital to our company's future. And we can redefine a firing offense to include employees who intentionally block change, or are unsatisfied critics, or even bullies.

Sales organizations do artificial selection all the time. People who can't figure out how to make the monthly quota get fired. But imagine applying this thinking to every single job in the company. What if there were a quota for everything and we measured ourselves against those quotas every day? Would that be helpful—or a disaster?

Quotas are worse than useless unless they're accompanied by control. Entrepreneurs profit from measuring themselves because they have the power to do something about the measurements. Smart managers know that measuring everyone also means giving the people being measured the power to do something about what they learn.

Jack Welch at GE has taken a lot of heat for his policy of requiring every manager to rate his or her staff and then (with a few exceptions) fire the bottom 10 percent of every group. Some view this as uncivilized and inhuman. Jack's response is that it's far

---

"Quotas are worse than useless unless they're accompanied by control."

---

better to fire someone after a year at the company than it is to carry them along for twenty years and then fire them, when it's too late for them to get another great job.

More important than pruning his ranks, Jack's artificial selection policy has a huge impact on the people GE has an opportunity to hire. People who are afraid of being in the bottom 10 percent are far less likely to apply. He's breeding a group of supermanagers.

Runaway Times Ten

Companies that know how to zoom will attract employees who want to zoom. Companies that can zoom are more likely to evolve, more likely to be successful, more likely to be launching

---

"When your company starts hiring zoomers, it's going to zoom faster!"

---

innovative new products and services. Employees who want to zoom are too impatient to work at companies that are slow and doomed.

When your company starts hiring zoomers, it's going to zoom faster!

And as it zooms faster, it will evolve. And it will find clients and customers who want to zoom with it, who will embrace its business practices and brands. And this, in turn, will only cause the company to evolve ever faster.

As some companies get better at evolving faster than the competition, those companies will be further disturbing the status quo, encouraging the zoomers to zoom faster. They'll make ever more turbulence, which will kick even more dust into the eyes of the companies that can't keep up. Some of the companies will figure out how to zoom and work to catch up. The rest will become extinct.

A quick look at the semiconductor industry proves this point. As the pace of development in computer chips and memory chips started to increase, it forced competitors to innovate faster or to fold. Those that chose to get faster created even more development, which caused their competitors to speed up as well.

This same arms-race mentality happened in the world of high-end stereo equipment. A sleepy little marketplace, it came unglued about ten years ago. Speakers got more and more exotic, with each entry leapfrogging the others, leading to an ever-increasing cycle of new models and new prices (you can now spend a hundred thousand dollars on stereo speakers and still not buy the top of the line). A company like Vandersteen, which makes a perfectly good, reasonably priced speaker, saw its market share decline because it was unable or unwilling to participate in the race.

The first people to leave the slower companies will be their best employees, their fastest employees, the ones who know how to zoom. And those employees will join other, more nimble companies, piling on and increasing the head start of these zooming companies. When they do this, the slow company they just left has still fewer chances to succeed. A negative feedback loop has taken over, with each employee defection making the company less fun to work for. It becomes more and more likely that the fastest people will leave. The race is over. (At least until the zooming competitor gets complacent and forgets to zoom. Then a newer and more aggressive organization will enter the race and raise the stakes once again.)

Companies can take advantage of this phenomenon or they can intentionally screw it up. Many companies that zoom to a head start intentionally start hiring nonzoomers because they want the company to settle down and start taking profits. At the same time, many companies that fall behind do everything they can to encourage their zoomers to leave.

Consider the case of Nancy Weinmaster, a senior scientist at Dial, the soap company. Nancy's the kind of person who gets excited about inventing a new skin-moisturizing lotion. Nancy is extremely good at her job, and exactly what Dial needs if it wants to create a new generation of products (and the profits that go with it).

In an economic downturn, though, Dial responded by hunkering down and spending less money on new-product development. Nancy, who carries extremely valuable memes, ought to leave. The project she has been working on is being shelved—along with 75 percent of the other products in development. Dial now faces a negative runaway . . . the best zoomers are fleeing.

A faster company will be lucky enough to entice Nancy away from Dial. That will make this company faster still, and Dial even slower. As faster companies introduce new products, Dial's products will fall even further behind. Management has a choice between two runaway cycles, one positive, one negative.

Is Incremental Change Enough?

We love "eureka!" moments. The legend of the inventor running through the streets, having just discovered a breakthrough, is the model for how things change in our world. If we need these giant leaps forward to succeed, how can incremental evolutionary progress possibly be a valid success strategy?

In his book *The Innovator's Dilemma,* Clayton Christensen calls these eureka events "discontinuous innovations." He points out that incremental change in big companies sets them up to fail when the really big things come along.

There are a few ways to answer this valid objection. The first is straight from Darwin. Given enough time, incremental evolutionary progress will invent quite extraordinary organisms. It took quite a while to evolve a zebra, but it worked.

Your response might be, "Sure, it took a long time to evolve a zebra. But evolution didn't have a competitor who could use a much more straightforward approach to create a zebra faster!"

You're right. That's why the second argument is more important. Loosening up companies, making their mDNA more plastic at the same time they implement fast feedback loops, makes it far more likely that the wisp of a good idea actually gets executed. Most of the noteworthy discontinuous innovations (the "aha" big ideas) that have rocked the business world did not originally come from start-ups. Nor were they top-secret, unknown ideas. Instead, they came from the research groups inside big companies that were too rigid to do anything with them. Only after they were ignored by their creators were entrepreneurs able to jump on them and take advantage of the hole in the marketplace.

For example, Nintendo, a Japanese company with a background in playing cards, appeared to come out of nowhere to create the video game machine that changed everything. But it was Warner's decision to abandon Atari and to ignore its founder's pleas to innovate that left the door open for Nintendo.

The Internet is heralded as a giant leapfrogging innovation, but virtually all of the important work on the structure and use of the Net came from the military, big universities and big corporations like IBM. AOL, Yahoo, eBay and Hotmail all happened because big companies declined to capitalize on their head start and take the market when they had an easy opportunity.

Once an organization overcomes the antichange fear reflex and gets good at small changes, the bigger changes are far easier

---

"The challenge companies face is not in inventing new ideas. It's in moving the old ideas out of the way so that they can implement the new ones."

---

to swallow. If you don't freak out when they move your parking space or change the color of the company logo, it changes the way you approach the big changes that come along.

The challenge companies face is not in inventing new ideas. It's in moving the old ideas out of the way so that they can implement the new ones.

My third response is that discontinuous innovation is overrated. Huge profits are made every day because of progress in areas where continuous innovation rules. Things like fashion, user interface, retail management and smart marketing contribute the lion's share of growth and profits. While advances in the laboratory make good stories, real profits can be captured by something as simple as making a car with cup holders.

Get the incremental, continuous innovation stuff right and the bigger, scarier innovations are likely to take care of themselves.

Chapter 6

WINNING STRATEGIES, GETTING UNSTUCK AND SEX

> The enemy is a stuck winning strategy and our reliance on command and control tactics that don't work any longer.
>
> Organizations can respond to competition and environmental shifts by organizing to evolve their mDNA, making incremental evolution less painful for the people who work there. If this happens, then in times of rapid change they will always defeat organizations staffed by people who view memetic change as a form of death.

Typing in France

If you've ever tried to check your e-mail while in Europe, you know about the nasty surprise I encountered on my last trip. Sure, it's fine with me that they speak French in France . . . after all, it's their country. But why did they have to mess with the keyboard!

The keyboard on French computers is intentionally messed up. You need to press the shift key to type a period, for example. Some of the letters are where they should be—making it even more annoying.

If I didn't know how to type, this wouldn't be a problem. When you're a hunt-and-peck typist, you're busy looking at the keys. So if someone intentionally screws up a perfectly good keyboard, you hardly notice.

But if you've figured out a winning strategy for typing fast, you're doomed. You mean to type www.thebigredfez.com and out comes zzz,thebigredfew,co, which is truly exasperating.

I used to be a good typist. I used to be able to surf the Net quickly and easily and well. I don't want to give that up. I enjoy my

---

"Getting comfortable with a winning strategy makes it incredibly difficult to embrace change."

---

competence. When I get to France and have to take six steps backward, I get frustrated.

My point is that getting comfortable with a winning strategy makes it incredibly difficult to embrace change.

The Winning Strategy

Every company with more than one employee has discovered a winning strategy. It has succeeded at something that gave the founder enough confidence to hire someone.

When I say "winning strategy," I don't mean that the strategy is perfect, or market-dominating or even good. Just that the strategy makes the founder (or the long-time CEO) feel like a winner. It's a strategy that generates results that the people at the company want to repeat again and again. The winning strategy encompasses the habits and decisions that are not up for discussion every day. When Henry Ford thought that it was more profitable to only make cars in black, that was part of the winning strategy. Today, of course, Ford couldn't care at all what color you want your car—it's not part of their core beliefs any longer.

Big companies got to be big companies because they had a powerful and profitable winning strategy. The little shop around the corner, despite delivering only a meager living to its proprietor, also has a winning strategy, one that the owner sticks with.

At many organizations, the winning strategy is astoundingly simple and well known by all concerned. At others, it is quite subtle and far more mysterious. Either way, every company still around today has a winning strategy or is about to go broke defending an old one.

Virtually all of a company's existing mDNA comes from its current approach to the business—the strategy that made the company successful in the first place. Not only is the winning strategy baked into the company's policies and assets, but the people who work at the company are there because they liked the winning strategy enough to join the company. Replacing a strategy that's still working is difficult indeed. However, if a company doesn't replace its strategy until it is completely obsolete, it will find that it has neither the time nor the money to find a new one.

Schwinn, the company that made the bikes you likely grew up with, is a great example of this trap. It had a winning strategy— exclusive bike shops and heavy, well-made bikes, produced in the United States. When the market shifted and people started buying cheap, lightweight bikes at the local Kmart, Schwinn was unable to alter its strategy in time and went bankrupt.

Why are companies so loath to abandon what's working today? There are several good reasons. The first is that following someone else's path is often an excellent substitute for the perceived risk of original thinking. If your predecessor has discovered a strategy that works, you don't have to come up with one on your own—that might or might not work better. Managers are not personally responsible if they do nothing except what's been done before—but if they take initiative, then it's their responsibility.

The second disincentive is that sticking with tried-and-true approaches helps justify past decisions. To try something new is, at least partially, to denigrate something old.

The third reason is that until recently, feedback loops were slow and unreliable. If you don't have vivid, immediate proof that your winning strategy is broken, why bother going through the pain of fixing it?

Let's look at it from the beginning. Any company—*every* company—goes through the same process (at first).

The new company flounders until it finds a winning strategy. This is the strategy that lets the company make payroll, make a profit, perhaps even grow. A winning strategy is fixed in that it doesn't usually change from day to day. It's not always rational but

---

"Managers are not personally responsible if they do nothing except what's been done before."

---

it's always based on history. Managers develop a superstitionlike attachment to the strategy, believing that it is responsible for the company's past and its future.

If you want to teach a pigeon to be superstitious, put it in front of a bird feeder that dispenses food whenever the pigeon pecks it. You'll discover that the pigeon painstakingly repeats all the motions that preceded the pecking—the bird doesn't distinguish between the activities that caused the food to come out (the pecking) and the ones that just happened to be performed the first few times (the twirling or preening).

Management superstition is similar. It's not unusual at all to find large pockets of management in complete agreement about what has worked for their company in the past (and what they expect will work in the future) based almost entirely on superstition.

For example, without any data at all, most people in the segment of book publishing that creates science fiction and fantasy novels believe that you must have a drawing of the hero on the cover of a novel or it won't sell. It's part of their winning strategy, it has been for a long time and they're in no hurry to find out if it's actually valid.

When a nascent company finds a winning strategy, the people who run the company pile onto that winning strategy bandwagon. Everything they do, they do in support of the strategy. They make rules to ensure that they maximize the winning strategy. They embed those rules into the company with their hiring choices, their real estate choices, their manufacturing choices, their policies.

As long as the winning strategy stays the same (and the competitive environment stays the same), the company thrives.

If this sounds a little like evolution in animals, it should. The DNA in a species is constantly being shuffled with and fiddled upon, and then one day, an organism springs forth that's ideally fit for a certain ecological niche. The combination of competition and environment is a perfect match for the winning strategy of this animal. So the fit animal piles on, generating tons of offspring. The population explosion continues until the competitive environment changes.

The cheetah had a winning strategy—run the fastest. It worked great until man invented the rifle and the helicopter. Betty Crocker had a winning strategy as well—make it easy to bake a cake at home. It worked until working moms discovered that they didn't even have time to turn on the oven.

Sooner or later, every winning strategy stops working. The competition catches up. Technology changes. The founder quits. When that happens, one of two things occurs: Either the company has enough time and enough guts to try to find a new winning strategy, or it fades into extinction.

Both are accompanied by a great deal of running around, hand wringing, layoffs, task forces and frenzy. And, with surprising predictability, neither approach succeeds.

This didn't used to matter very much. A good winning strategy lasted for a few generations, enough to build a family fortune or at least deliver a great career. Today, though, because the rules change so often, winning strategies don't last for long.

Companies that understand their winning strategy have taken the first step in identifying the pillars that hold that strategy together. Turkish Air, the national airline of Turkey, for example, has a winning strategy of flying people into and out of Turkey. No surprise there. But it's instructive to note that the strategy is limited to planes and to Turkey. If people suddenly don't want to fly into and out of Turkey, the airline is in trouble. It would face similar trouble if planes were replaced by something faster, safer or more convenient, or if the price of fuel increased by 500 percent in one year.

Discovering your winning strategy and saying it aloud is critically important in getting ready to change it. The easiest way I can describe for finding your strategy is to do this: Figure out what changes in the outside world would be the worst possible things that could happen to your company. (No fair picking something that affects every business . . . it's got to be something that is specific to your industry.)

NBC could lose its viewers to alternatives like cable and the Net. Procter & Gamble could lose customers to lower-priced generics if consumers decided that there was no real difference among products or if they stopped watching commercials. StarKist could discover that there are no tuna left in the ocean. Starbucks would be rocked by a report that caffeine causes sudden, uncontrollable cerebral hemorrhaging. In each case, understanding how bad luck (or a competitive threat) could upset the apple cart brings the winning strategy (and a company's dependence on it) to the fore.

The winning strategy is at the heart of a company's mDNA.

Especially at the beginning, all of the policies, procedures, staffing and assets of a company are aligned with this strategy. If the winning strategy changes but the company fails to change its mDNA, stress sets in, followed soon thereafter by failure.

The Stuck Winning Strategy

Before your company has a chance of adopting a posture of zooming, you need to understand why you are stuck in your current winning strategy. Only then do you have a chance to undo the deep aversion people have to abandoning something that they believe is working.

Why are entrepreneurs able to accomplish tasks that leapfrog big companies? Entrepreneurs have no winning strategy to replace, so they're far more open to finding one. They're less critical of apparent imperfections and are willing to grab (and run with) the best available new strategy.

Your winning strategy is built around a meme. Then, you and your colleagues build all sorts of new tactics to support that core meme. Replacing your winning strategy requires more than just changing the original meme—you've got to rebuild all the tactics as well. And that's a daunting task.

Your company's current winning strategy isn't perfect. You may think it's forever, but it's nonoptimal, impermanent, filled with holes and inefficient. But it's yours! The idea of switching to an unproven model—one that has obvious drawbacks and plenty of risk—is way too scary (and too much work) to get excited about. After all, there is little or no cost to sticking with what you have. You won't have to lay off anyone tomorrow. You won't have to hire unknown people, go to fundraising meetings or take responsibility. You can happily leverage someone else's proven model.

Unfortunately for you, there are always more entrepreneurs gunning for you. Unfortunately for you, the changing world will always give someone open to finding a new winning strategy plenty of angles that make their newly adopted strategy more powerful than yours.

In the formative years of our industrial economy, there was enough stability that you could ride a great winning strategy for several generations. Build a great steel mill or car factory or patent a formula for correcting mistakes on typewritten docu-

---

"Unfortunately for you, the changing world will always give someone open to finding a new winning strategy plenty of angles that make their newly adopted strategy more powerful than yours."

---

ments and you had it made. There are all sorts of cultural institutions (from big factories to retirement plans) that reinforce our belief that winning strategies should last a long time. Today, though, the life cycle of a winning strategy is shorter than ever, meaning that allowing your current strategy to get stuck is costing you money.

In the "old days," the life cycle of a winning strategy was plenty long enough. You could start a job, have a career and practically retire before the winning strategy failed. The prospect of having to abandon your strategy in mid-career was met with terror, not glee.

Today, of course, the strategies are coming faster and faster. Worse, they're often discontinuous. There isn't always a new winning strategy waiting to take off at just the right moment. ARCO, for example, was an oil company known for being analytical and smart about applying that analysis. They invested hundreds of millions of dollars in solar power when they sensed the winning strategy of sucking every possible drop of oil out of the ground might be coming to an end.

Alas (for all of us) their timing wasn't so good. The technology of solar didn't respond to the money invested by ARCO, at least not in time for them to develop a new winning strategy that could replace the old one. Bad timing for ARCO, but of course, evolution doesn't care.

Part of the wisdom of conglomerates like 3M or GE is that with multiple winning strategies working at the same time, they can layer the tails of the strategies so that one is hitting its peak just as the next one is fading out. ARCO didn't have that luxury, because they're in only one business.

Even a conglomerate, though, is not organized to replace a particular winning strategy at the optimal moment. It's human nature not to seek out a replacement before you need one.

Competent People Embrace the Current Winning Strategy

Most people like to think that they're competent. Competent people have a predictable, reliable process for solving a particular set of problems. They solve a problem the same way, every time. That's what makes them reliable.

Competent people are proud of the status and success that comes with being competent. They guard their competence, and they work hard to maintain it. Top-down command and control managers like to have competent workers.

Bob Dylan, on the other hand, zooms. From year to year, from concert to concert, there's no telling what he'll deliver. Sometimes, he blows the world away with his insight, his energy and his performance. Other times, he's just so-so. The one thing that's certain is that he's going to change.

The factory-centric model of work caused us to adopt Six Sigma quality-management systems. These data-driven approaches to quality are fine as far as they go, but they tempt us to turn workers into competent automatons. We're trying very hard not to let anyone be Bob Dylan at work.

Thanks to our work at creating competence, the receptionist can no longer lose your messages, because they go straight into

---

"Competent people are proud of the status and success that comes with being competent. They guard their competence, and they work hard to maintain it."

---

voice mail. The assembly-line worker can't drop a tool, because it's attached to a numerically controlled machine. The telemarketer who interrupts your dinner is unlikely to overpromise, because the pitch is carefully outlined on paper in front of him or her.

Today, it's much harder to make a bad car, because robots are measuring everything. It's much harder to be an incompetent directory-assistance operator, because computers are handling so much of the work.

As we've turned human beings into competent components of the giant network known as American business, we've also erected huge barriers to change.

In fact, competence is the enemy of change!

Competent people resist change. Why? Because a new winning strategy threatens to make them less competent. And competent people like being competent. That's who they are, and sometimes that's all they've got. No wonder they're not in a hurry to be Bob Dylan.

Piling On to the New Winning Strategy

Smart companies realize that big successes are often the result of luck, and that there may be a long time until the next one. So they're good at piling on.

Piling on is an art. Hasbro knows how to do it, and so does Warner Records. When you release a product that's on the verge of breaking through, you need to mobilize every asset you have to leverage it.

Every year at Toy Fair, the big toy companies introduce far more products than they expect to produce. Toy Fair is held in February, nine months before the peak of the Christmas toy-buying season. This gives the manufacturers a simple luxury: Make the stuff that was bought by the stores and cancel the stuff that failed.

By discovering a new winner and then piling on with all of their resources, the toy makers are able to take many chances early while limiting their risks later on.

Harry Potter is another example of piling on. Scholastic releases hundreds of books a year. They're awfully good at using their winning strategy (books for kids through a variety of channels) to hunt for breakthroughs. But after the success of the first Harry Potter book, Scholastic knew they didn't have the skill or the assets or the resources to push the character as far as he could go. So they sold the entire brand to Warner. All the marketing rights (except for books) now belong to the movie studio.

Warner is pulling out all their stops. They're piling on. If they're right, they'll generate hundreds of millions of dollars in profit. You may not like what they do to Harry (why did they change his glasses?), but they will take the winning strategy and milk it for all it's worth.

Knowing when to pile on (as AOL did once ICQ started to succeed) or when to abandon ship (as Amazon did with their Junglee shopping service) is an art.

Extinction as a Way of Life

Imagine that you have two elephants, a male and a female. Elephants have a very long gestation cycle and only one offspring at a time, so the species is noteworthy for how long it takes them to reproduce.

If there are no casualties—if every birth is a live one and every elephant lives a life of average length—how long will it take for the descendants of this pair of elephants to dominate the entire surface of the earth? The answer, according to Charles Darwin, is less than five hundred years. Every few years, the population of elephants would double. And doubling gets you to big numbers very quickly.

Obviously, almost everything dies before its time. If it didn't, we wouldn't have room for all the elephants. If every business that was started this year survived, we'd run out of people to staff these companies in just a year or two. If every project initiated by your company was a success, you'd be the biggest employer in town within three years and the biggest company in the world in five.

Extinction is part of the process of creation. Failure is the cornerstone of evolution. With the vast majority of new products and initiatives going down in flames, the best strategy is not to assume

---

"Failure is the cornerstone of evolution."

---

the best, it's to assume the worst. Assume that almost everything is going to fail and you'll be right. As long as your realistic thinking doesn't turn into negative thinking that increases your likelihood of failure, this approach guarantees that you'll launch more initiatives more often.

One of the reasons "hot" companies cool off is that in the middle of their runaway success, they become too proud to fail. They're too successful and too busy harvesting their success to launch new initiatives that are more than likely to fail. As a result, when the current success falters (as it always does), they're not ready with something to replace it.

When a company or a project enters runaway, management has just a little time to use the cushion that came with that success to launch new projects. What an opportunity! Take the innovators who were responsible for the last success and encourage them to try again—there are plenty of less imaginative managers who can take their place running the current successful venture. Don't believe your own press releases and put all your assets behind these new ventures—they'll probably fail. But try often enough and you're likely to find yet another runaway success.

Most companies in the computer industry are one-hit wonders. They develop a product, it works and then they milk it for all it's worth. The structure of stock options is one reason (as long as you can keep the stock rising for four years, you win), but the other reason is pride. Software folks know how random success can be, and there are plenty of good personal reasons not to risk one success by following it up with a failure.

Sexual Selection at Work

There's an odd species of bird at the Bronx Zoo called the cassowary. The male's head is covered by a small helmet made out of the same thing as fingernails (keratin). My six-year-old son thought it might be for motorcycle safety (always wear a helmet!), but it's probably something that evolved as a result of sexual selection. Female birds really get excited about the helmet. The male birds with big helmets are more likely to mate and thus pass on their genes.

When the big-helmeted males and the helmet-loving females give birth, the new females are also likely to be helmet-loving (it's genetic), and the males are far more likely to have big helmets (because their dads did).

Over time, the helmet becomes more and more common until just about all the male birds in the species end up with big helmets. Some have *huge* helmets!

But what's the helmet good for? What possible evolutionary reason could have led to the creation of this bizarre, wasteful (from a survival point of view) growth?

In fact, it's because the growth is wasteful that it is useful. It turns out that only very fit birds, birds with extra resources, could possibly find enough internal energy to grow a helmet. The sick birds, the struggling birds, the birds with mutational deformities—all would be hard-pressed to grow a helmet. The lack of a helmet serves as a signal to the females: This guy is a loser.

Animals need these signals to allow them to communicate fitness honestly. If they didn't exist, unfit males (who have nothing to lose) would lie about their fitness and happily mate, passing on genes that weren't as fit as their competitors.

It turns out that a similar process exists in organizations. Why do big companies allow their purchasing agents to be visited by highly paid salespeople in fancy Italian suits? Shouldn't they ask the companies to fire the salespeople and give them a better price instead? Why not refuse the golf games and the seats at the U.S. Open? Why do we respond to big booths at trade shows?

The answer comes from Darwin. The companies that can waste the time and money to send these signals are the ones that we believe are more likely to have the resources to provide good customer support, more likely to be in business years from now.

The dot-com mania that swept our markets through the late nineties was characterized by a signaling strategy that was unique only because of its excess. There were hundreds of venture-backed companies, all looking to get enough traction to file for an IPO and go public. Since it wasn't revenue or even traffic that was making a company a candidate for overnight riches, how did a smart executive maximize her chances of success?

For more than two years, the signaling strategy of choice was to waste as much money as possible by signing up for a sponsorship with AOL, Yahoo! or another web portal. Ideally, the amount of the sponsorship would be larger than the competition could spend, and the media purchased would be as unmeasurable as possible. The more overpriced and useless the media, the better.

Why? Other than enriching stockholders at AOL and Yahoo!, what good did this strategy do? It was a grandiose signaling scheme. Competitors, investors and employees thought, "If a company is well-funded enough and gutsy enough to do a deal *that* big and *that* dumb, well then they're probably well-funded enough and gutsy enough to end up as the market leader." If enough people agreed, it might just become a self-fulfilling prophecy.

This is not irrational, just as peacock mating rituals are not irrational. For a time, it gave potential investors, partners and customers an excellent insight into the aggressiveness and leadership tactics of a company.

It's very easy for an entrepreneur or a salesperson to want to ignore signaling strategies, especially if they're able to offer a product or service that's demonstrably *better* than the competition's. Yet it's often the suits or the trade shows or the full-page ads or the backgrounds of the top executives that send the signals that really matter.

Executives in the book business look first to the reputation of a literary agent before they read a novel that's being submitted. Physicians considering whether to test a new drug are certainly influenced by the marketing track record of the pharmaceutical company behind it. Signals matter.

When I took my first job at a company called Spinnaker, I drove my stuff from California to Boston to get to the company's headquarters. Along the way, I dropped a friend off in Chicago. Leaving the city, I passed a huge billboard for Spinnaker!

I was floored. I was twenty-four years old, the thirtieth employee of the company, and they were already running billboards around the country. It filled me with pride and enthusiasm to think that I was working for a company that hot.

Only when I told this story to the president of the company the next week did my bubble burst. Turns out that Chicago was the site of the annual Consumer Electronics Show, the big event where all the purchasing agents from Target and Kmart and Wal-Mart made their choices about what was going to get stocked next Christmas. And Spinnaker had purchased a billboard (just one) strategically located on the way from the airport to the convention center.

Did Spinnaker executives really think that someone would be persuaded to buy their products because of their logo on a single

---

"Apparent overspending on high-leverage signals may be the best investment you make in a new project."

---

billboard? Of course not. But they were exactly right in their prediction that it would serve as an effective signaling strategy for the buyers who came to the trade show (and one new employee who happened to stumble on it).

So, the imperative is to plan for failure, to repeatedly try new winning strategies and to do it as cheaply as possible. Yet, at the same time, don't try to skimp on your signaling strategies. Apparent overspending on high-leverage signals may be the best investment you make in a new project.

Six Ways Companies Can Use Signaling Strategies

1. Have a very fancy reception area so that potential employees will be more likely to accept your job offers.

2. Hire an extremely well-paid, highly esteemed executive, regardless of price, if the presence of that executive signals the gatekeepers at crucial clients or backers.

3. Run intentionally wasteful direct mail campaigns that reach very small numbers of influential targets. Send signed leather hardcover books by Federal Express to the fifty people you most want to seduce.

4. Fire a profitable client in a very public way.

5. Hire a beautiful receptionist.

6. Pay your receptionist $10 million in bonuses for no good reason.

The goal of each of these strategies is to waste money, but to do it in a way that brings the maximum impact. Because if you waste the money the right way, you're not really wasting it, are you? All too often companies waste money indiscriminately. The genes of those cassowary birds could start growing toenails all over their bodies, after all, but it certainly isn't going to impress the female of the species.

Of course, in some environments, fitness may not mean demonstrating how successful you are. It may instead involve showing how frugal you are. So you could signal this to potential employees by doing all your interviews at Starbucks, and demonstrate it to your customers by delivering your goods in a plain brown bag, shipped priority mail. Being so extreme in your lack of

---

"The lesson of the cassowary is that sexual selection is as important as natural selection in creating interesting species. Sending fitness signals efficiently saves you time and money and, more important, leads to better mates and more offspring."

---

wastefulness is a form of waste in and of itself (it's hard to concentrate at a Starbucks), so the very irrationality of it serves as a signal.

Signals aren't right or wrong. Instead, they either work or they don't. Signals that give a company an edge over the competition that is worth more than the cost of the waste are probably worthwhile. Signals that show bad judgment (putting money in a wheelbarrow and lighting it on fire) are probably a waste.

The lesson of the cassowary is that sexual selection is as important as natural selection in creating interesting species. Sending fitness signals efficiently saves you time and money and, more important, leads to better mates and more offspring.

Your Most Important Sex Is with Your Boss

As individuals, we know far more about ourselves than anyone else does. We also know more than we put to use. Unfortunately, we're not encouraged to be honest about our strengths and weaknesses and ways we want to contribute. In fact, we're subtly encouraged not to be truthful about what we're not good at.

In order to get people to embrace change, the office has to be not just safe for people to admit what they don't know, but unsafe for those whose conduct discourages change.

How does a company balance every manager's obligation to hit key deliverables (this month's sales quota, this number of widgets out the door) with a need to experiment and fail? The easy answer is to make zooming one of the deliverables, one of the things that is measured along with the "real" deliverables. This isn't going to happen just because one top executive orders it. Instead, it will take brave bosses who start small and invest in their employees and make zooming a requirement for job success.

How do you create a company culture that encourages change, especially in established companies? Why does nothing from Saturn translate at GM? A company's leaders and their memos may say over and over that they value innovation, but that can be an old, meaningless saw. Instead, bosses (and eventually, senior management) have to live it. "Culture" as it is practiced

---

"In order to get people to embrace change, the office has to be not just safe for people to admit what they don't know, but unsafe for those whose conduct discourages change."

---

in many companies, is overrated, while the importance of the day-to-day interactions between employers and employees are underrated.

Every time you interact with someone at work, you're swapping memes. And the most important meme-swapping goes on with your boss, because you know that your survival (your job) depends on it.

Top-down policies are not the best way to create a zooming organization that learns to evolve. Instead, it's the meme-swapping, the hallway conversations, the small signals that will create the environment that allows this to happen.

If the memes you're swapping with your boss aren't dramatically enhancing your personal mDNA and making it more likely that you'll succeed, it's time to find a better boss.

Embracing New mDNA

Sexual selection is a major driver of corporate evolution, and one way to change mDNA in a hurry is through an acquisition. By acquiring another company, you can dramatically change the way your company behaves. Alas, far too many acquisitions fail. The reason has nothing to do with the strategy behind the acquisition. Instead, it comes straight from the evolution of animals: It's no fun being a lion cub.

Most prides of lions consist of a bunch of females (usually sisters and cousins) and one dominant male. Male cubs are welcome to stay with the pride until they stop nursing (which takes a year or so). After that, they have to leave and find their own pride.

The king of beasts services his harem and is master of all he surveys. Except, of course, when he's challenged by another alpha male. If the dominant male loses to the challenger, the challenger takes over the pride. No surprise there.

What happens next is shocking (but not surprising after you analyze it). Within thirty days, all of the lion cubs still with the pride will be killed by the new dominant male.

Why? Because a nursing cub ensures that a lioness is infertile. This delay in the new male's ability to impregnate the pride means that it will take longer for his genes to pass on to a new generation.

Given two imaginary lions, a gentle one who waits until the

cubs are older and an aggressive one who doesn't, the aggressive lion will spread more of his genes, faster. That means, of course, that aggressive genes have spread through the lion population, creating male lions who kill cubs as a matter of course. Selfish genes spread faster. The gentle gene is no longer part of the lion gene pool.

Precisely the same thing happens at many companies. The CEO or her strategic task force identify a company and acquire it. They then hand it over to an operating executive with instructions to integrate the acquired company. The problem is that the new company has mDNA, but it's not the operating executive's mDNA.

All too often, the executive begins by looking at the products or services the acquired company brought with it. All of these products (like all products, everywhere) are imperfect in some way. All embody trade-offs. The executive sees threats. He sees products that don't carry his memes. It's easy to criticize these products, of course, and easy to kill them off.

Now the executive is left with a bunch of employees and few products. He didn't hire these employees, and like all employees, they're imperfect. The most senior employees, the ones most likely to have a significant impact on the company, probably made a lot of money in the acquisition and they're in no mood to play games with this executive. They can't bear to see their genes stamped out, so they leave. This leaves other employees, employees whom the manager has no stake in seeing succeed. If they leave, he can hire new employees to replace them—employees who are beholden to him, chosen by him and carrying his mDNA.

Just as the alpha lion killed all the cubs so that his genes would spread faster, the executive kills all the products and fires all the employees so that his mDNA spreads faster.

Does this mean your company should stop doing acquisitions?

SURVIVAL IS NOT ENOUGH

Not at all. For many companies, acquiring other companies is a key step in evolving their mDNA. Remembering that the reason you did the acquisition is to acquire mDNA may help your management team hesitate before they go out of their way to eliminate the very thing you just bought.

Consider this example from McDonald's. It's hard to imagine a company with better-defined and more consistent mDNA than

---

"Remembering that the reason you did the acquisition is to acquire mDNA may help your management team hesitate before they go out of their way to eliminate the very thing you just bought."

McDonald's. It has one giant brand that looks very similar the world over, and it dominates an industry that it invented.

Two years ago, McDonald's acquired the struggling Boston Market roast chicken chain. The reason was simple: It wanted the real estate. The idea was to fire everyone, stamp out the evil mDNA and build other restaurants where Boston Market used to be.

The company promoted Jeffrey Kindler, who was the top lawyer at Boston Market, to CEO, and put him in charge of the transition. His job was to renegotiate leases and gradually shut down the Boston Market stores. He had a different plan, though.

Just a year later, Kindler—who had no previous restaurant management experience—completely turned Boston Market around. In fact, Boston Market stores have increased their sales at double the pace of McDonald's stores. And McDonald's is no longer planning to close down the brand and move on.

In fact, the brand is expanding—with an agreement with Heinz Foods to put Boston Market entrees in supermarkets. Boston Market is now the only non-McDonald's brand that is succeeding inside McDonald's. Rather than killing the acquired company's mDNA, McDonald's is watching Boston Market's mDNA spread. Kindler was just promoted to be in charge of *all* their non-burger brands.

If the goal of an acquisition is the mDNA, not the product line, then treating that mDNA like an asset is more likely to lead to success. Treat the acquired people like heroes. Give them important, executive positions. Listen to their opinions right away, not in a year or two after they've proven their loyalty.

Sex Is Important

Evolutionary biologists continue to debate the origins of sex (it's much more efficient for an organism just to split like an amoeba or clone itself without risky and expensive copulation), but despite the murky origins, the vast majority of visible creatures have sex in order to procreate. Even bacteria have sex on occasion.

Sex accomplishes two things. First, it allows the DNA from two organisms to combine in their offspring. Sex is an essential tool for gene transmission. This seems like the obvious outcome, but it couldn't happen if organisms didn't find other organisms to swap with.

A chromosome swap is very similar to what happens when a company hires someone. If a struggling company goes outside the firm in search of a new CEO, people call that "looking for new blood." It's not too far wrong. When the new CEO shows up, a frantic exchange of mDNA begins.

The senior executives of the company work hard to spread their memes to the new CEO. They show her the way they "do things around here." They try valiantly to impress the CEO with their strategy, their policies, their past decisions and their projects.

At the same time that the CEO is being injected with these memes, the CEO has her own agenda. She was hired, after all, because of her experience, insight and smarts. So she's trying to figure out which of her memes to bring to the company and, just as important, which people are going to stay and which carry such bad memes (and have such stuck winning strategies) that they have to go.

The second thing that sex does is largely overlooked but is at least as important. It cancels out mutations. In nature, the vast majority of mutations are not positive. The average human being is born with at least one significant mutation out of the thirty-five-thousand genes he or she carries and if those mutations were passed on unchecked, we would have a much higher rate of birth defects. When we mate, though, the sex process finds many of the errors introduced by mutations and corrects them before they're passed on to our children.

The same thing happens at a company. If a new employee can't adopt the company's winning strategy, if he fights with the memes held most dear by the company, it's not unusual to find that person shunted away from a position of authority, or worse, fired. Put ten engineers on a team, as we've seen, and their teamwork will weed out most of the negative mutations. Meme recombination works very much like genetic sex . . . the outliers disappear.

This is the time to remind yourself of Muller's Ratchet. In an isolated pond, an organism that reproduces without sex is often busy evolving into extinction. Why? As we saw earlier, in all species, most offspring have DNA that is likely to contain a few new mutations. But, in this case, since asexual reproduction doesn't cancel out mutations as well, they become part of the offspring. The result is that over time, harmful mutations accumulate, and in many cases, the species becomes dysfunctional and disappears.

If you spend eight years writing a biography and no one reads it until it's done, it's likely it's not nearly as good as it could have been. You've probably embedded the same errors deep throughout the entire book. If someone had commented on your first chapter, you would have caught those unwanted errors (the mutations) and eliminated them from the rest of the book. Have sex or get stale.

By exposing your organization to people carrying memes you'd like to incorporate, you're likely to lose some individuality (the

---

"Have sex or get stale."

---

mutations will be shunned), but you'll benefit by gaining memes from the talented people. The challenge is to choose which memes you absorb and which you discard.

Companies tend to have committees (who work to maintain the status quo under the guise of increasing communication) and teams (who are assigned to actually accomplish something). Committees are bad because they eliminate all mutations, even the good ones. Teams, on the other hand, can be a very useful way of swapping mDNA and removing bad mutations at the same time.

Removing a person from an organization, while it doesn't have a direct analogy in animal genetics, is a form of sex as well. Now, however, instead of *adding* that person's memes to the mDNA, you're deleting them. This form of corporate sex is one of the most powerful available to management. There's probably no faster way to alter a company's mDNA than to fire the right people.

Artificially Selecting the mDNA in Your Company (aka Firing People)

Just about everyone knows a bully at work.

Bullies are annoying, difficult, counterproductive, and sometimes even dangerous, yet nobody actually seems to want to do anything about the steady supply of new bullies who emerge on a daily basis. A bully is a person who uses external force to entice others to do things his way, regardless of what a rational person might say is the best course of action.

The bullies we feared growing up were physical bullies. They used their perceived greater strength (or our perception that they were willing to use it) to get whatever they wanted.

Unfortunately, bullies don't stop bullying when they grow up—they just learn to hide it better. A kid who learns to get his way by bullying isn't going to abandon this winning strategy just because he or she has a job.

A bully gets what she wants at the expense of the group's well-being. And because bullies operate from a zone of fear, they're the most likely to effectively oppose change of any kind.

Bullies can keep your company from investing in a profitable new area because they're insecure—and unsure how it will affect their career. They can ruin the career of a promising new upstart because they view that person as a threat. Bullies can make it hard for other companies to do business with you. Most of all, bullies make it hard to zoom.

Why are we willing to tolerate bullies? I chalk it up to fear and ignorance: fear that if you stand up to a bully, you'll somehow hurt

---

"Bullies make it hard to zoom."

---

yourself and the organization, and ignorance about the best way to deal with the bully. The thing is, most bullies are bullies because they're scared. And that means that they're among the first people who will stand in the way of your quest to institute constant change as a way of life.

A bully-free company is faster, smarter, more profitable and more fun. Stand up to the bullies. If they quit, fine. You'll survive. And if you replace them with nonbullies, the company will thrive.

Firing people is dramatically underrated as a management strategy. By firing people who slow your company down, you're doing a dramatic service to everyone who's still there. Sticking by one or two powerful people who refuse to zoom can easily lead to the layoff of 2,000 people.

Years ago, Ken Olsen, the founder of Digital Computer, steadfastly refused to embrace both open systems and the personal computer. His board of directors should have fired him. Instead, they indulged his obstinacy and saw the entire company fade away and then be sold for scrap.

Is there someone with influence at your company who frequently stands in the way of change? What would happen if that person left?

Choose Your Customers, Choose Your Future

Your customers do a lot to determine your company's mDNA. If you're a PR firm that represents crazy, impulsive superstars, you've organized and staffed to make yourself good at dealing with crazy and impulsive superstars. If you didn't, there's no way they'd stay with you. At the same time, though, it's unlikely you've evolved your skills and staff and assets to make your firm the ideal choice for a boring corporation. Just down the hall in your building, on the other hand, is a firm that represents the Russian Orthodox Church, Exxon and the Washington Philharmonic. Odds are that they'd last about five minutes if they had your client list.

Every time you interact with clients, you swap memes with them. They affect the work you do, the prices you charge, the rate at which you change and the kind of person you hire.

Years ago, my company's biggest client (accounting for nearly 50 percent of our sales) was a big, loud, pushy, angry company. The people who worked there pushed their suppliers hard, trusted no one, broke their word frequently and were not the easiest people to please. We were dependent on their income (and the word of mouth it generated would bring us even more income), but our interactions with them were changing our mDNA. We were hiring differently, interacting with each other differently, and most important, interacting with our other clients differently.

I had no choice. I fired our biggest client.

The alternative was to become a firm I didn't want to become. The alternative was to evolve into a company that specialized in insane deadlines and cranky clients.

Some customers demand suppliers that are deeply entrenched in maintaining the status quo. They demand a level of predictability

---

"Every time you interact with clients, you swap memes with them."

---

and staffing that will make it very hard for you to build a zooming company. Thus, you choose your future when you choose your customers.

If you determine that your future success as an organization lies in your ability to adapt to changes in the competitive environment, then you'll need clients that agree with you. Every time you take money from a client, you're swapping mDNA, and if their mDNA is slowing you down, you're trading your future success for today's revenue.

Chapter 7

SERFS, FARMERS, HUNTERS AND WIZARDS

Change is not monolithic. Different sorts of employees create different sorts of change. One of the main reasons organizations fail to change is that they try to introduce the wrong kind of change at the wrong moment.

The Danger of Role Models

As I write about different kinds of companies, the temptation is to use real-life examples, to talk about companies that are doing it right, and then to describe, in exhaustive detail, precisely how they do what they do.

The danger is that during times of chaos, today's role model is tomorrow's disaster. The very thesis of this book—that change is everywhere and no one can predict what's next—makes it difficult to make safe choices when searching for the perfect example.

Ten years ago, these organizations, for one reason or another, would have been on anyone's list of exceptional companies: AMF, Baldwin Pianos, Candies Shoes, Chiquita Brands, Converse, Danskin, Florsheim, Friendly's, Fruit Of The Loom, Grand Union, Hilton, Lechters, Loews Cineplex, Mary Kay Cosmetics, Pep Boys, Polaroid, Rand McNally, Revlon, Rite-Aid, Saks, Samsonite, Sunbeam, Vlasic Food, and Xerox. Today, every single one of them has stocks or bonds trading at junk or near junk levels.

Three years ago, the poster children were decidedly more

high-tech. Companies like Ask Jeeves, drkoop, Engage, Juno, Net-Zero, Quokka, theglobe.com and Webvan were the talk of their industries. Each had a stock that was soaring, all were reinventing the world as they saw it. If you were looking for a bold new way to think about business, this was a great place to start. All of them have stocks trading for one dollar or less as I write this.

So, benchmarking anything other than an attitude and a process is a dangerous game. We need to start somewhere, though, so to make my points about different kinds of employees I'm going to use elements from two companies: Amazon and AOL. I've chosen them because they take very different approaches to the challenges of evolving, and because I've had personal experience with both. I don't believe that new media has cornered the market on innovative thinking, but since this is the most chaotic industry of all, it's easier to look there for the most striking examples of change. Just as evolutionary biologists prefer to use fruit flies and *E. coli* for their experiments, Amazon and AOL are perfect because of their fast evolutionary cycles.

Amazon Tweaks and Tests While Wal-Mart Struggles

Wal-Mart used evolution as their secret weapon to catch up with and eventually overtake Kmart. Sam Walton set out to test and measure his way to success, and the strategy worked. Thirty years later, Wal-Mart realized that they needed an online store if they were going to continue their growth and capture dollars that were moving online. But rather than learning from Sam's success, they ignored his strategy when it came time to go online.

When Amazon started, the company had nothing to lose. Its founder, Jeff Bezos, had just a few employees with some cheap office furniture, holed up in Seattle. No reputation, no venture capital.

Starting with little, Amazon experimented like crazy. They had nothing to slow them down, so the first site went up in just a few

---

"When Amazon started, the company had nothing to lose."

---

weeks. There was no warehouse because Amazon outsourced that. The customer service department was staffed by the few people who also worked in marketing and accounts payable.

Every day, Amazon tested and measured and improved. Over time, they gradually added features, acquired companies, closed and opened new stores. They evolved.

Wal-Mart started later. Much later. And the mindset of the Wal-Mart team was not surprising. They told me that as the world's largest retailer, they had to think big. They realized that after their site went up, it would be visited by huge numbers of people, so it had to be robust. And because people had come to expect one-stop shopping from their Wal-Mart store experience, it also had to be complete.

After one aborted launch, they actually took the site down for a month while a new executive retooled it for a second launch. That rebirth has been unsuccessful as well.

Success hurt their ability to zoom. Wal-Mart fell in love with their permanent winning strategy of low prices, mass scale and underserved communities. This is the strategy that made them a star. (They forgot about the testing and measuring part that led to these memes).

When they decided to launch an online store, they assumed that their current offline winning strategy would work without any changes. They assumed that they could dictate the terms, and that their huge brand and reach would take care of any problems that arose.

How much has Wal-Mart learned from the online experiences they've had? Compared to the systems that teach them how customers behave in their stores, essentially nothing. Wal-Mart isn't evolving fast enough online, and until they do, they're likely to continue to fail in this medium. They have a fixed winning strategy online and it's stuck.

How could Wal-Mart have avoided this fate? My advice would have been to launch a small site, with perhaps ten products for sale. Make the offers on the products as remarkable as possible (remarkably cheap prices or remarkably well-written offers or remarkably high-demand items). Build a permission asset so Wal-Mart could talk with these early customers and test new offers. As word of mouth spread, set a small team loose on both evolving those ten offers and adding new ones.

Imagine that instead of selling every book, as they do now, they choose to just sell *The New York Times* top ten bestsellers (Wal-Mart stores sell more *New York Times* bestsellers than any other chain in the world). Instead of selling a wide range of clothing, why not just Wrangler jeans?

By creating offers for specific products, by understanding—through actual doing—how the processes work, Wal-Mart could create a platform for change.

Over time, the people at Wal-Mart would learn what was working and repeat that throughout the other parts of the site. Imagine saying to a team of ten people, "Each of you gets ten pages. Tweak them every hour until you figure out what approaches get the highest yield." At the end of a day they'd have tested eight hundred different offers. And from that sort of knowledge, Wal-Mart could grow and continue to evolve its online business with confidence.

Serfs, Farmers, Hunters and Wizards

There are four types of people in most organizations:

Serfs do what they're told.

Farmers work within the bounds of a winning strategy but use feedback loops to constantly improve the efficiency of their efforts. It's very similar to natural selection—see what works, do it more.

Hunters work a company's existing winning strategy, but expand it in ways that probably hadn't occurred to management. This is sexual selection—seek out the best matches and get those genes hooked up with yours.

Wizards introduce significant mutations into a company's mDNA, creating opportunities for entirely new winning strategies. Wizardry is like mutation. It's not usually the most reliable survival strategy, but a good mutation can change a species forever.

While the connections to evolution are clear, the correlation among these four types and various job descriptions is not. There are cashiers who are acting like wizards and hunters while there are CEOs working for Fortune 500 companies who are serfs. It's an attitude and a skill set, not a hierarchical ranking.

Farming, hunting and wizardry all represent different ways in which companies that are zooming can evolve.

Continuous improvement is a form of farming. Organizations have successfully implemented Six Sigma programs and other feedback systems that make it easier for their employees to constantly improve upon the status quo.

There's a difference, though. Unlike Six Sigma or other forms of continuous improvement, farming can be subjective and it can be quite widespread. I don't believe there's a foundation task at most companies that can't be farmed to improvement. While a Six Sigma program has, by definition, an end goal (you can't top 100 percent quality), farming never ends in its quest for better yield.

The second form of evolving is hunting. This involves broadening a company's winning strategy through larger shifts than farming can. A farming organization is far more likely to be successful at hunting—and far more likely to actually implement the results.

The third form of evolving is the noncontinuous jolt that comes from wizardry. It takes a wizard to see that a company ought to reinvent itself on top of a new technology or by acquiring a fast-moving but smaller firm. Companies that are already fluid, that have already built themselves around the ideas of farming and hunting, are far more likely to make these jumps than companies filled with serfs.

Little changes are good practice for big changes. Once you learn that little changes won't kill you, big changes aren't as scary. So many companies that are stuck (but profitable) want a wizard to come in and tell them what to do—and then expect their middle management to persuade the serfs to embrace a brand-new way of doing business. The problem with this vision is that it doesn't work. It's painful at best and a complete disaster most of the time. It's much more natural to evolve constantly than to undergo painful shifts on a regular basis.

The zooming organization that reaches runaway becomes unstoppable when it comes time to implement the wizard's

---

"Little changes are good practice for big changes."

---

changes. Why? Because the company is filled with people who work there because they want to, people who have intentionally rejected their role as a serf in a different organization and are thus primed and motivated to zoom, to embrace the new winning strategy.

The Life of a Serf

McDonald's isn't picky about who they hire, partly because they have little choice (turnover is very high) and partly because they've optimized their machines and systems to be operated with little or no training.

By investing a fortune in machinery, McDonald's has dramatically decreased the percentage of local labor necessary to put a hot meal on a tray. They'd rather do the work in a factory in Chicago than let the teenagers in your town do it. For excellent short-term economic reasons, McDonald's succeeds when it treats the people working in the store just like cogs in the machine. Like serfs.

The goal of most large companies is to pay serfs as little as possible, all the while working to replace them with machines. Fifty years ago, for example, AT&T was on a pace to hire half of all the women in the United States to work as telephone operators. Besides the fact that this was impossible, it was becoming a huge cost center for them. The first step was to streamline the hiring and management process so that operators could be sourced cheaply and paid very little. The obvious next step was to invent

---

"The goal of most large companies is to pay serfs as little as possible, all the while working to replace them with machines."

---

large mechanical switches that would replace the operators with a machine that worked for free.

We see this again and again. In *Fast Food Nation,* Eric Schlosser describes efforts of the fast food industry to build automated devices that will eliminate as many human steps as possible in the creation of a burger. There will always be a need for serfs—in fact, at any give time, most of the headcount in a company is composed of serfs—and companies will always be working to eliminate the jobs that they currently fill.

As we automate, serflike jobs migrate from traditional blue-collar roles (such as auto assembly) to white collar ones (such as insurance adjuster). It now takes the Ford Motor Company a smaller number of man-hours to assemble a car than it did just twenty years ago. Yet we're not seeing massive unemployment. If Ford needs fewer workers to make a car, but employment on the whole is rising, where are the new jobs coming from?

The new blue-collar workers no longer hammer rivets. They don't work at US Steel—they work at Aetna. Their jobs have changed, but they're actually quite similar. Instead of banging the same rivet into the same hole all day long, workers are now required to type the same numbers into the same spreadsheet all day long. This will continue until Aetna figures out how to find a reliable (and cheaper) robot to do the typing.

While we associate low-paying jobs with serfdom, that's not always the case. There are millionaire investment bankers who work as serfs, as well as well-paid commission salespeople who use the standard script and the standard company PowerPoint presentation as they take orders for a hot product all day long. Serf is not a pejorative term. It's merely a description of the worker's role in the company. Serfs do as they're told. They are dependable cogs in the company machine.

Why Do Companies Hire Serfs?

Why do so many people want to be serfs and why are there so many companies eager to hire them?

Our genes drive us to work in a steady job that insulates us from a lot of external change. The goal of our genes is to be well-fed and to avoid being eaten or killed before we procreate and raise successful children. Having a strong boss and working in a successful company is a pretty safe way to do that (it appears).

Do what the boss says and you won't get fired. If you don't get fired, you'll eat tonight. For many people in many cultures, this is the ideal scenario. We overlook the fact that we're not intellectually challenged in exchange for the certainty that our job is secure.

The reason companies hire serfs instead of driving them to do more than follow orders is that the machine-centric view of the enterprise demands it. If your organization is a giant machine, controlled from the top, then it needs to be filled with human cogs, each playing a role as reliably as possible.

If a company is going to grow and wants to have a wide span of control (lots of people working for just one boss), then it needs to have manuals and rules and policies. Without a decision-making boss standing over each employee, it's impossible to control a large workforce without policies.

So a bargain was struck. Companies want to leverage their winning strategy and do it without reconsidering each policy constantly, while many employees want the security that comes from following instructions. The governmental-industrial complex could never have been built without the active cooperation of the people who work there. Companies like the top-down dependability. Employees like the feeling of security.

The End of the Serf Era

Constant turbulence in the markets means that the security that serfs traded for is no longer present. Employees may like the feeling of security, but security is gone. We read of layoffs of three thousand or eleven thousand or two hundred thousand workers at a time. The only way a company can lay off that many people at once is for most of them to be serfs. If Motorola shuts a plant, most of the people they fire are good, hard-working employees, doing exactly what they are told and following the manual.

Of course, volatility has been around for as long as there have been jobs, so this by itself is not new. At the same time that we're further eroding the social contract, though, corporations are also learning how to measure.

Fast feedback loops mean that a supervisor can know within an hour if a telemarketer is doing well tonight. Fast feedback gives people on an assembly line constant updates on whether or not they're being productive.

A fast feedback loop is a simple concept—knowing as soon as possible whether something is working or not. When you drive a

> "A fast feedback loop is a simple concept—knowing as soon as possible whether something is working or not."

car, you find out within a split second if the brakes are working— either the car slows down or it doesn't. Technology now makes it possible to get feedback on ever more tasks, and to get that feedback faster than ever.

Combine the two—turbulence that leads to insecurity and the ability to measure everything—and being a serf is not what it used to be. It's now a one-sided bargain, and the serfs are starting to wise up.

Transforming Serfs into Farmers

For companies trying to evolve, a large number of serfs is perhaps the largest single impediment to change. While it seems simple to make changes to an employee handbook or to quickly announce new policies, the reality is that changing the behavior of large numbers of serfs is hard.

Why? Because your company has spent the last generation teaching them not to change. "When I want your opinion, I'll give it to you" has been the watchword of factory-centric management for a century, and changing that overnight is extremely difficult.

In companies that are struggling with change, a large serf class is frequently one of the forces dragging the company, forcing it to act more slowly.

What should be done? I'm not proposing that companies lay off tens of thousands of people. Far from it. The challenge is to

---

"In companies that are struggling with change, a large serf class is frequently one of the forces dragging the company, forcing it to act more slowly."

---

transform the organization's mDNA and allow loyal, hardworking employees to produce far more than they've previously been allowed to.

It starts, as we've seen, with zooming. Changing all the time, often with no specific goal in mind—just to get good at the process of making tiny changes without getting stressed about it.

There's a purpose to this, though. Once you know how to zoom, you can farm. An employee who is able to make small changes can now put a focus to those changes, can start making those changes toward something.

Fast feedback loops can cause a workforce to move from unquestioning serfs to always probing farmers. American Airlines can turn their telephone operators into farmers. How? They can review how long a caller was on hold before the phone was answered. They can see in real time what percentage of callers ended up booking a ticket. They can intercept the calls that don't lead to a ticket and have a supervisor (or a computer) ask the caller what the problem was. Better yet, instead of management handling the feedback loop, they can give it to the operators. Give them the data and the freedom to do a better job.

Take it even further. American can make it easy for someone on an airplane to call corporate headquarters *during the flight* to give feedback about good or bad service, about a pilot who drones on and on about invisible landmarks down below or a flight attendant who goes the extra mile to pacify a screaming child.

Putting those feedback loops to work, American could turn many of its serfs into farmers—employees who use feedback to independently change their actions and improve their performance. They could create an environment in which individuals are rewarded for constantly (and consistently) modifying their behavior in order to increase whatever is being measured.

We act like serfs because we're genetically attuned to it, socially motivated to do it and often have no choice because of limited job opportunities. The combination of rapid change with technology, though, is going to take a big chunk out of the size of the serf population, pushing many of these workers into (potentially) more fulfilling and higher-impact jobs as farmers.

Let Some of the Serfs Work Somewhere Else

Just a century ago, Henry Ford built a dynasty by vertically integrating. He turned iron ore into steel in Michigan and owned sheep farms in England where the wool for seats was produced on Ford looms. Ford's business model was simple. He was paid to be a manufacturer, so the more of the manufacturing he did, the higher his return.

Today, Bob Lutz, the former vice-chairman of Chrysler, is building a $100-million sports car company with just twenty employees. It will create the Cunningham without owning a factory, without making tires or steering wheels or even assembling the cars. Astoundingly enough, he'll earn far more per car than Henry Ford ever dreamed of.

Lutz isn't going to be rewarded by the market for manufacturing prowess. He doesn't want to be in a low-return serflike business. Instead, he's getting paid for design and insight and marketing.

And it's not just the car business. Baskin-Robbins no longer makes ice cream, Coca Cola outsources much of its bottling, Motorola didn't make that cell phone in the pocket of your jeans (which Calvin Klein didn't make).

Kudos to Boeing for moving its headquarters to Chicago. By moving senior management away from the factories of their division in Seattle, the company makes the factories less visible. It forces senior management to evolve without the daily reminders of the tens of thousands of people just next door making airplanes.

The problem with serfs is that they will inevitably slow down your business. You will always have undersupply or oversupply, and it will be your problem, not someone else's. There's no question

"The big successes will go to those who can evolve faster and leverage more valuable assets."

that adroitly managing a serf workforce can generate a profit. But that profit will continue to shrink, while the big successes will go to those who can evolve faster and leverage more valuable assets.

Farmers Know How to Tweak

Farming didn't suddenly arrive on the scene. Mankind didn't go from picking berries and hunting woolly mammoths to plowing fertile soil overnight.

Instead, farming evolved. The first farmers probably did nothing more than discover that the seeds of various trees and plants, when they fell off their muddy clothes, would later grow into useful sources of food. Aborigines in Australia discovered that setting fire to a section of marsh or grassland would create (a few months later) a region of tender shoots that would attract rodents and marsupials, making hunting easier. Endless improvements and constant tweaking made farming efficient.

The artist Grant Wood would have us believe that farmers are dour, boring and afraid of risk. Actually, the opposite is true. Farming yields worldwide continue to soar, largely as a result of a relentless cycle of testing and measuring. Because a change in yield can make the difference between a successful harvest and one that loses money (or leads to starvation) farmers have understood for thousands of years that focusing on yield is their most important activity.

Farming only works in populations that know how to imitate. Teaching your goldfish to juggle doesn't do all the other goldfish any

---

"Farmers have understood for thousands of years that focusing on yield is their most important activity."

---

good—one fish's learning doesn't transfer to any other fish. Establishing the communication and follow-up mechanisms that permit farmers in your company to talk to each other and teach each other isn't cheap, but it's necessary if you're going to farm your processes.

Amazon Knows How to Farm

There are countless examples of farming at work. Amazon.com is a company staffed with farmers. Because Amazon knows the results of every page, every e-mail, every price point, they can (and do) test and measure whatever they do.

Amazon knows to the penny what they are paying for traffic. They have computed the lifetime value of an ideal customer, and every single person who buys media for the company knows all the numbers. At one point, Amazon shared the numbers with their vendors, telling them, "If you can beat this number, we'll buy unlimited ads from you."

Unlike other sites around the web, which change their pages every forty-four days on average, Amazon is in constant flux. On a given day, 10 percent of the people visiting the Amazon home page might see an experimental new directory layout, while the other 90 percent see the same old thing.

In February 2000, for example, Amazon completely overhauled its tab system, replacing it with text links that resembled those used by Yahoo. You probably never saw this experimental

---

"If your boss is more likely to say, 'we'll work it out' than 'you're fired,' you're going to be more likely to try new things."

---

page—it didn't work and they abandoned it. Getting it wrong is just as important as getting it right, though, as it showed a willingness (even a passion) for testing.

Sam Wheeler is a point man for Amazon's new business development. When Amazon is launching a new effort, they put someone like Sam on the case. After the launch of their new ebook site, Sam responded to my long laundry list of constructive criticism with a simple mantra: "It's early. We'll work it out." And they did. Day by day, week by week, the kinks disappeared. They farmed that section of the site to make it better and better.

As a result of this farming mindset, Amazon is more willing to take risks and launch new ventures than most companies. If your boss is more likely to say, "we'll work it out" than "you're fired," you're going to be more likely to try new things.

QVC Outfarms Amazon

In the year 2000, QVC did more than $3.5 billion in sales, with their best day topping $55 million. Selling by television, direct mail, over the Net and with a few products in stores, QVC is a retailing powerhouse. On a good day, three hundred thousand phone calls come in to the company, and 180,000 packages are shipped.

QVC realizes that they only have 24 hours of airtime a day. As a result, they've worked hard to maximize the value of every moment. A QVC producer knows, on a second-by-second basis, how a given product is doing. If it's doing well, he can keep it rolling. If not, he can quickly cut to the next item in the queue. Most products are guaranteed just seven minutes of airtime. After that, it's up to the farmer running the control room to decide what happens next.

At the same time that QVC is farming the airwaves, the company realizes that if they do nothing but maximize today's profit, there will be no growth tomorrow—so they test more than 250 new products a week. That's at least thirteen thousand tests a year.

With that sort of appetite for new products and new ways of presenting them, the company is constantly looking for new memes that work. Their record day, for example, involved the sale of more than $40 million in Gateway computers, something they never would have attempted during their earlier days.

Note that QVC doesn't own any factories. They can quite happily let others develop products and take financial and production risks. As the company that ultimately connects to the consumer, they get to keep most of the profit.

This lack of factories means that they can turn on a dime. If Razor scooters are going to be hot, QVC can have them on the air a few days after making the decision.

At the same time, QVC's ability to farm is limited by their customers. The QVC customer, one of the company's biggest assets, also slows their ability to change. How? By having a fairly rigid set

---

"The QVC customer, one of the company's biggest assets, also slows their ability to change."

---

of expectations. People who watch QVC have an idea of what to expect, and they tune in with a certain experience in mind. In order to generate revenue, QVC has to resell its customer base every single day, and if they go too far out of the box of what its customers want (selling life insurance, for example) they'll fail.

Think Like a Waiter

A few years ago, I met a senior advertising executive, someone who should have known better. When we sat down for coffee, the first thing he asked me was, "What's direct marketing?" At the time, I was too stunned by his ignorance to give a cogent answer, but I've thought long and hard about it since, in case it happens again, and here's my definition: Direct marketing is measured, action advertising, delivered straight to the person the marketer has targeted to take that action.

Super Bowl ads aren't direct marketing because the advertiser doesn't expect the viewer to take action right now as a result of the ad. Billboards have a similar problem, plus they're pretty hard to target. Every single ad run on the Internet, on the other hand, could/should be a direct marketing ad.

That said, what if everyone in your company could be in a position to think like a direct marketer? Direct marketers are very focused people. They pay so much for stamps and printing and inserts that they can't afford to just let a failing campaign ride. If it's not working, they pull it. Immediately. Direct marketers are also obsessed with fast feedback. Finding out if your ads are working is the single best way to save money—no sense running a bad ad next week if you know today that it didn't work last week.

This is all fine and good for selling insurance or coffee, but how does it affect your company? Think for a minute about the quandary of a restaurant owner. Most of the time, the owner can't be in direct supervision of people who are waiting tables. There you are in a fancy restaurant and someone who's making just a few dollars an hour is serving you. Imagine how hard it must be to get those underpaid servers to provide a level of service commensurate with the eighty-dollar check you're about to get.

But what about the tips? Great question. I believe the reason restaurant service in the United States is as good as it is (from Denny's to Lutèce) is that waiters think like direct marketers. At the end of every meal, the waiter finds out how he did. Even if most people tip 15 percent regardless, a big tip can make a waiter's day, so like it or not, the waiter is paying attention.

Over the course of a week or a year, good waiters figure out which actions get them good tips. They may not do this consciously, but the fast feedback loop in place makes them more likely to repeat actions that work and to avoid those that don't. Waiters who can't figure out how to work the system usually stop being waiters.

For all the people in your company who are farmers, you need a system just like this—fast feedback loops that inform employees (and their bosses and peers) how they're doing. Here's an example:

Many people in white-collar jobs spend all their time interacting internally. They send internal memos, generate internal e-mail, run internal presentations and meetings. And most of the time, these people have no idea at all if they're doing a good job. They have no feedback loop (save a vague annual review) that lets them know if they're having a positive impact.

What if there were an e-mail system that changed that? Let's call it Dynamemo. Dynamemo could track internal e-mail in the following way: It would allow recipients of e-mail to rate the quality of what they just read, the same way Amazon lets you determine if a book review was useful or not.

Over time, e-mail from people who have previously sent e-mail that wasn't highly rated would drop to the bottom of your inbox, so you could avoid those people if you chose (a great incentive to rate people and to do it right). And on a regular basis, the folks who sent internal mail could get aggregated feedback on how they were doing.

If you discover that no one thinks your mail is useful and fewer and fewer people are reading it, you'll take action. Or you'll get fired. Either option is better than annoying people with your failed attempts to communicate.

Note that just like tipping or direct mail, this system is constant, consistent and subtle. It doesn't involve the tense annual review loaded with negative (but constructive) criticism. Instead, the feedback loop is one that a farmer wants to hear: when you do that, this happens.

Successful salespeople force this process to occur. They call it closing the sale. Instead of taking "I'll think about it" as an answer, these salespeople realize that a "maybe" is as good as a "no," so they might as well push for a final answer. By getting these answers sooner, they're able to adjust their pitch to create one that gets better results. They farm the system. Now, with technology, we can create similar feedback loops for almost any interaction.

People in your company are likely to resist this feedback loop. Direct marketing, after all, accounts for only half of all advertising, even though the other half is an unmeasured crapshoot based on faith and sizzle. Why? Because marketers don't like to be measured, especially when they're spending someone else's money. Feedback loops aren't your friend unless you are really serious about farming with increased yield.

Hunters Don't Own Land

The biggest difference between a hunter and a farmer is that the hunter's winning strategy has far more freedom built in. A farmer can experiment and tweak, but sooner or later he lives and dies based on what comes out of the ground he tills. A waiter can't switch restaurants from day to day, so his arsenal is limited to changes he can make in a very small range. A hunter, on the other hand, is always moving around. If this territory isn't paying off, he can move to another one.

This increased freedom makes it likely that a hunter is going to be more aggressive in expanding his winning strategy. After the immigrants who became Native Americans arrived by land bridge from Russia, it took them only a few thousand years to drive 85 percent of the large animals in North America to extinction. As hunters, they were able to quickly evolve new techniques for killing animals that were new to them.

The best examples of hunters in the business world are sales-people. They too are frequently driving successful strategies to extinction and are always on the lookout for new methods and new territories.

Salespeople with a diverse product line and a large territory are able to develop an astonishing range of techniques for identifying

> "Because salespeople often know within a few min-
> utes of making a pitch whether they've succeeded,
> they're able to test more often."

prospects, arranging meetings and closing the sale. Because sales-people often know within a few minutes of making a pitch whether they've succeeded, they're able to test more often. These fast feed-back loops mean that a sophisticated salesperson can radically and frequently change his approach, searching for the one that best expands his business.

Hunters also have the luxury of owning no milking cows—so they have more time to roam than a farmer. In exchange, though, the hunter has a responsibility to report to the people who depend on him so they can plan the food supply, and just as important, to report to his peers so that they can learn better techniques.

AOL Knows How to Hunt

During the mid-to-late 1990s, AOL knew how to hunt. Ted Leon-sis, a key figure in AOL's development, was a master at trying new things, all with the aim of increasing AOL's range and profitability. Ted started the Greenhouse project, aimed at bringing new online services into being. The Greenhouse prided itself on its speed at making decisions. Budding entrepreneurs would arrive at 10:00

A.M., make a pitch to the Greenhouse committee and then wait in the lobby. It usually took less than four hours for an answer to come back, and deals were signed within days or weeks. By rapidly seeding everything from the Motley Fool to NetNoir to Love @ AOL, Leonsis was able to discover and launch new content—without taking all the time, effort and money that would have been required in-house.

It was also Ted's idea to acquire ICQ, the instant messaging service that allows Internet users to send messages to each other in real time.

In addition to these large-scale hunting expeditions, AOL continually reinvented the way it generated money from advertising. A few crack salespeople had carte blanche to find new prospects and sell new deals. Once an approach worked, the rest of the salespeople were taught how to replicate it and instructed to use it over and over again until it ran out of steam.

Just as Amazon needs to spread the successful farming tips it discovers from one store to another, companies with more

> "Once an approach worked, the rest of the salespeople were taught how to replicate it and instructed to use it over and over again until it ran out of steam."

than one hunter need to work to increase the communication that goes on once they discover a successful technique. Hunters who don't share do nothing to improve a company's winning strategy.

Fast Feedback Loops for Hunters

In many companies, hunters don't naturally share their secrets, as it does little for their career and even makes it more difficult to maximize the value of a new strategy (your own colleagues be-come your competitors). In the case of salespeople, sales force automation software (SFA) tries to help.

The idea is simple. If the VP of sales knows the status of every account, every salesperson and every product, she can run a more efficient, more responsive organization. Alas, there are a few problems:

- First, selling is notoriously interpersonal, making it difficult to capture nuances in a database.

- Second, by the time a salesperson enters the data into a com-puter, it is either incorrect or out of date.

- Third, salespeople are encouraged to sell, not report, so most of the data is incomplete at best.

- Fourth, salespeople feel as though they "own" the client and don't want to give him up to the system.

Wireless technology is about to change this. Imagine a system in which a salesperson driving back from a sales call can call into the SFA computer system. Using voice recognition, the system asks the salesperson a series of questions, each question more probing than the last.

Now, the entire firm (from purchasing to investor relations) can get updates on order flow within minutes. Even better, the VP of sales can put the new knowledge to work in real time. It lets her adjust pricing on a hot product before too much time passes. It also gives her an opportunity to spread the memes from one hunter to another far faster than the competition.

Plenty of Companies Have No Clue How to Hunt

Remember, perfect is the enemy of good. In most companies, there are huge cadres of people who have investments in the current winning strategy and the status quo. They realize that successful hunting tactics will certainly increase internal change, making their day-to-day existence less certain. It's harder to be a serf in a world that discovers new strategies.

One company I worked with had perfected the art of farming in one medium. It knew exactly what to do in order to continually

---

"Perfect is the enemy of good."

---

increase its yield. Suddenly, a new medium appeared. The logical thing to do was to move into that medium as well.

Now, if you were starting from scratch, you'd enter the new medium slowly. You'd spend a few dollars, test some ideas, work your way up the food chain, discovering what worked and what didn't. This is how Lillian Vernon and L.L. Bean learned how to do direct marketing and how Caterpillar learned how to make tractors.

But when a successful company moves from one field into another, it forgets about doing things slowly. Instead, there is huge pressure to go big or stay home. Figure out how to do it perfectly, spend all the money you think you'll need, get buy-in from management and launch. The self-esteem of the company in one field is just too great for it to embrace failure in another field.

So this company has spent the last three years trying to perfect its strategy for dealing with the Internet. Long, fractious meetings end with rancor. It's logically impossible to reconcile two diametrically opposite opinions and still launch with unanimity. So it is doing nothing.

Wouldn't it be easier to launch both ideas, on a small scale, and see what happens?

Choose Your Employees, Choose Your Future

If farming is like natural selection and hunting is like sexual selection, then there are several kinds of sexual partners your hunters can find you: customers, employees, strategic partners and investors. We've discussed salespeople, but for most companies, the biggest driver of your future is in your employees.

If your company has 15 percent turnover (not unreasonable) it means that every six years or so, you've replaced the entire firm. You can choose to do this in a last-minute, panicked way, or you can realize that there's no better opportunity to define your future.

The usual HR strategy comes straight from the factory view of the world. If employees are nothing but cogs, then hiring the first person (or the cheapest person) who can do the job is the best way to go. Spend as little time and money as possible.

But if your worldview shifts and you believe that hiring changes your meme pool and gives your company the edge that can start you down the path to runaway, what could be more

---

"Great employees are the last great bargain."

---

important than hiring the right people? This is not a book about hiring (there are plenty of good ones), so we'll skip the tactics, but the lesson is to elevate the time and money you spend on this process.

I'm not arguing that you should spend a little more money on salaries or a little more time on hiring. In pursuing my strategy of being extreme in all things that matter, I'm suggesting that you spend two or three times as much on your HR staff as you do now, that you spend two or three times as much on identifying and hiring exactly the right people, and I'm suggesting that you fire ten times as many people next year as you did last year.

It's very easy to give lip service to HR. If you have a factory-centric view of your organization, then it has to be nothing but lip service. But if your goal is to build a runaway group of zoomers, how could anything be more important? Great employees are the last great bargain. Grab them while you can.

Wizards Invent

I love walking into a successful company and describing how it can use its assets to accomplish something very different—and helping it visualize how far this breakthrough will take it. Sometimes, I'm even right. That's what wizards do.

When we think of evolution, it's mutations that come to mind first. Mutations are the glamorous part of the science fiction view of evolution. A gamma ray creates the Hulk or a radioactive spider turns Peter Parker into Spiderman. Mutations are the big changes, the discontinuous changes that appear at the last moment and rescue the species from extinction.

Understandably, many companies crave the mutations that wizards create. *The Innovator's Dilemma* explains how many companies fall victim to technology changes that they didn't see coming (or couldn't take advantage of once they did see them).

The overlooked part of Christensen's theory is that it's not the knowledge the wizard has that's missing from many companies. It's the willingness to act on it. Microsoft could have purchased Palm, Apple could have licensed the Mac OS to clone makers, Western Union could have marketed fax machines and Sears could have put a Gap store into every one of their outlets.

Companies with successful winning strategies and very little zoomwidth resist the magic that a wizard can bring to their company. This is why continuous innovation and evolution set the stage so effectively for discontinuous change. If the company is always ready to try something new, if it's easy to propagate successful change throughout the company, the wizard will actually accomplish something.

If a wizard walked into your company, would you and your colleagues be able to adopt her ideas? Michael Bloomberg left Salomon Brothers and then launched the Bloomberg machine—a multibillion-dollar idea. Xerox ignored the folks at Xerox Parc who invented all of the elements now incorporated into Microsoft Windows. The list of companies that couldn't zoom enough to adopt an "unproven" idea is long indeed.

Yes, most mutations are not good for the species, and most of the things a wizard will bring you won't work either. But unless your company knows how to zoom, even the wizard's great ideas will go nowhere.

In Defense of Slack

In the battle between genes and memes in human culture, the genes will always have an advantage when lives are at stake. If the company is having trouble making payroll, it's often the new projects that get cut first. It's not an accident that the memetic revolution of the last thousand years closely matches the growth in leisure time that came with advances in the technology of farming. If "leisure" time is the time we don't spend surviving, then you need that luxury in order to have the ability to create and spread nonessential memes.

Alas, in tough times, it's the new memes that are going to save the company, not the old ones. This lesson comes hard to many organizations. When times are good, our inclination is to reap the benefits of our hard work, to sit back and take profits. When times are tough, the obvious course of action is to stick to the knitting, obsess over what we know, make payroll, take no "risks" and generally refuse to evolve. The end result is that few companies are as open to memetic change as they ought to be.

Tom DeMarco makes a persuasive argument for slack in his book of the same name. Slack is the unallocated time in your working day. If a company views its people as parts of the machine, there should be no unallocated time. Maximum efficiency occurs when everyone is busy all the time. But what does busy mean? If a group of knowledge workers have slack in their day, they're more likely to farm more frequently, or to create the interpersonal connections that lead to new efficiencies.

This leads to an ironic observation. The one thing that can save our organizations from distress and then death is memetic evolution. But that's also the one thing we're most likely to cut when times get tough.

The poignant aspect of this slash and burn approach is this: If a project fails, it's almost always the folks who worked on it who get

---

"If your company is nothing but a factory, then shouldn't we be blaming the architect—the person who designed the system—not the cogs in the wheel?"

---

blamed. But if your company is nothing but a factory, then shouldn't we be blaming the architect—the person who designed the system—not the cogs in the wheel?

In nature, natural selection drives a hard bargain. Mutations are given one chance to succeed—if they fail, the organism dies and the mutation dies with it. Natural selection can't see several generations ahead. It can't say, "Well, that nascent claw might be pretty useless now, but if we give it time to mutate and evolve in future generations, it'll really come in handy."

Organizations are different. We can provide our wizards and hunters the opportunity to develop the next generation of memes that will generate the huge profits we'll need during the next cycle and the cycle after that one. There are two caveats:

- *Be obsessed with low overhead.* As we've seen, expensive projects aren't more likely to succeed than cheap ones. The best way to give your experiments the room they need to succeed is to keep the costs of unproven projects close to zero.

- *Don't confuse a desire to zoom with a lack of responsibility.* Just as we need to be careful not to prematurely close down the work of hunters and wizards, companies must also hold them responsible. While natural selection in the animal kingdom is particularly unforgiving, this stern approach delivers a powerful result: The improvements that get through the screen really work, while the genes that can't improve disappear. The same approach can work in your company.

In most organizations, it's easier to launch an R&D project or hire a salesperson than it is to cancel the project or fire the salesperson. The manager who was delighted to spread the good news of adding to staff or finding a grant now has to share the bad news. And it's only natural to avoid the unpleasant stuff.

But if companies hesitate to shut experiments down or to fire nonproducing hunters, they'll inevitably get to the point where they're hesitant to launch many new memes as well.

When the posture of the company changes and the act of introducing a new idea is no big deal (because the act of canceling that idea is no big deal either), the number of ideas that get launched increases dramatically.

Consider web pages, for example. Some sites are quite proud of the fact that their home page has had a "consistent" look and feel for two or three or five years. They defend the way they're

---

"When the posture of the company changes and the act of introducing a new idea is no big deal (because the act of canceling that idea is no big deal either), the number of ideas that get launched increases dramatically."

---

interacting with visitors by pointing out that the consistency makes it easier for return visitors.

Meanwhile their competition is launching "inconsistent" new sites and interfaces all the time, and inevitably discovering better techniques, while the consistent site falls behind.

The alternative is to decide that every week your site will test a new home page on 10 percent of the people who visit your site. It's technically easy to implement, and the cost is nothing but the incremental cost of making a new graphic or two. The impact, though, is tremendous. Fifty times a year, your web group must now come up with a new way of interacting with consumers. Fifty times a year, they test something. Fifty times a year they learn something about what works and what doesn't.

Responsibility comes with this flexibility. If the group can't come up with a worthwhile approach every week, something's wrong. If the group can't beat the original approach every two months, something's wrong. Establishing the status quo and then setting time frames to beat that status quo is the smart way to manage this evolutionary process. It's not about waiting for a miracle. It's about expecting an evolutionary solution that works.

Slack isn't really slack. It's an essential investment in tomorrow's version of your company.

Chapter 8

THE BASIC BUILDING BLOCK IS PEOPLE

The most convenient carrying case for mDNA is the individual. Each individual has his own winning strategy and carries a large number of memes with him to every job and every situation.

The idea of zooming is so important, I've contributed a special section to the monster.com career site. Visit www.content.monster.com/zoom for more details.

It Starts and Ends with the Individual

The employee is the basic indivisible building block of the organization. Employees can be arranged into groups, divisions, offices and task forces, but ultimately, management now builds companies around people, not factories.

As I mentioned earlier, this gives employees far more power than ever before. Truly talented individuals are worth more, because when they move from one organization to another, they bring more value with them.

But this power also brings a huge responsibility to the individual. If your boss isn't giving you the opportunity to zoom, you have to protect your personal mDNA and leave for a job in which you can improve it. As the ultimate caretaker of your mDNA, every move you make affects it—increasing or decreasing its value. If you are nothing but a vessel for your memes, then allowing those memes to increase in value increases your value. You're the new "selfish gene."

Books and courses and public speaking all increase the value of your mDNA, as does the chance to lead projects, make sales calls or learn a new skill on the job. On the other hand, when you're in idle mode, your value compared to that of your peers decreases.

Selfish genes, of course, don't mean selfish people. The loyalty you show to your organization is often (but not always) the most "selfish" strategy you can follow.

Consider two friends who graduate from business school (or college or high school) on the same day in 1984. Bob takes a great job but quickly gets slotted as a serf. He makes a decent living and incrementally advances through his company. Today, he's a vice-president. As long as Bob's company has a winning strategy that's working, Bob will be safe and happy.

Frank, on the other hand, moves from job to job, mating with companies and swapping mDNA as he goes. For the first few years, he's got less power and less income than his friend from school. Then, suddenly, a gap appears. Frank has evolved his mDNA to the point where he's worth far, far more than his old friend.

Bob was able to leverage his serf status at a big company for a while, but now he's stuck. The company is fading. He's added little value to his mDNA and has little power. Frank, on the other hand, is in a position to write his own ticket, largely because he invested early and often in his asset.

Evolution is going to come to your company from the bottom up. People like Frank understand that their days are too valuable to spend sitting still. In order to attract and keep employees who can move a company where it needs to go, companies have to permit employees to zoom.

The implications are obvious. Smart, talented employees will work to maximize the value of their mDNA. Smart, talented bosses will work to find and keep those smart employees, and they'll do it by creating companies that insist that people zoom.

Changing Your Personal mDNA: Bad News from My Sister

After my sister finished her first two years at Carnegie Mellon, she got a summer job. I was thrilled for her. Then I heard where she was going to work: the Social Security Administration.

I imagined my sister Emily, filled with enthusiasm and fresh mDNA, walking into the biggest bureaucracy the world has ever known. She'd never have a chance. She'd be infected with their memes. She'd quickly evolve her first (and most important) winning strategy around the heartless, mindless, policy-laden world of the Social Security Administration.

I was heartbroken, eight weeks later, when she received the intern of the year award from her office. Not only had she adopted their memes, but she'd done it so well that they'd given her an award!

As an employee, it's hard to think about your job as a stopover on a lifelong journey of personal evolution, but that's exactly what it is. Whenever you take a job, you bring your mDNA to work and

> "Whenever you take a job, you bring your mDNA to work and it interacts with the mDNA of the organization and everyone else there."

it interacts with the mDNA of the organization and everyone else there. You learn to evolve your winning strategy so you can succeed at your new job. You learn about what works and what doesn't—both internally and externally.

And when you leave, you don't forget everything you learned.

The learning you take with you—the changes to your mDNA—is a double-edged sword. On the one hand, you're smarter and more sophisticated than when you went in. On the other hand, you're going to bring those strategies to your new job, and most of them are going to be useless at best, dangerous at worst.

The two jobs that have the most impact on how you'll do in your next job are your first job and your most recent job. Your first job sets expectations and lays down winning strategies that will stay with you until the meme is forcibly removed. Your last job got you this job, and you expect that your new employer will want the memes you just embraced.

The good news is that Emily was deprogrammed, and she was able to develop a new winning strategy before it was too late. Now she's quite happily marketing high-tech devices in Massachusetts. The bad news is that all of us (including me) grew up with first jobs, second jobs and last jobs that were built around the idea that change is bad, that our companies (and the people who work there) live and die around today's paradigm. We are all carrying around mDNA that encourages us to avoid change—at the very least, to push change off until tomorrow.

In order to build a zooming organization, we need to deprogram ourselves. The zooming organization is not just a clever label or something that you can use to kick off the next corporate offsite. Instead, it's a fundamentally different set of memes about how we do business. It's a different winning strategy for each employee and for the organization. And it's a very different hiring and firing strategy.

I've worked hard to sell you on the need for abandoning a winning strategy that you may be quite comfortable with. I know it's hard to give that up. The good news is that once you adopt the continual change that comes with zooming, it's easier to evolve and you'll be more likely to succeed.

Once you've decided to zoom, to adopt increasingly more powerful winning strategies to advance your career, you find yourself in a powerful position of searching for a better boss.

Find a Great Boss

The factory-centric model of industry puts the corporation in charge. Without a factory, after all, there is no business.

Today, though, employees have most of the power, particularly employees who are talented and willing to zoom. When you see the world this way, the challenge is no longer for the company to figure out how to use people the best possible way—instead, it's up to the employee to find a great boss and figure out how to use the company the best possible way. A chicken is just an egg's way

---

"The challenge is no longer for the company to figure out how to use people the best possible way—instead, it's up to the employee to find a great boss and figure out how to use the company the best possible way."

---

of making another egg—and a company is just a job's way of making a better job.

If you're in a company that treats you like a serf, your first step ought to be to try to persuade your organization that zooming is a better strategy. If that fails, leave. Find a company that wants you to farm, to develop, to find better memes and to spread your own.

Why is it up to you? Why can't your company fix your job? Your career mDNA is your responsibility. Every job you take, every project you lead and every person you interact with affects your career mDNA, building an asset you own, you control and you profit from. Companies don't work as well from the top down. You have to manage the change up.

Choosing a job is a far bigger decision when you see it in this light. Instead of focusing on how you're going to make next month's car payment, you now see that this job is going to affect your opportunities and benefits at the next ten jobs you take.

The same is true about choosing to stay with a job. I have friends who are paralyzed by dot-com stock options that are now worthless. The fear that someday these options might be worth a lot of money is keeping them glued to their desks, toiling at a job that is no longer improving their mDNA.

Two years from now, when they finally realize that waiting for the money was a mistake, they will have lost two years of opportunity. Two years of learning and career growth and enhanced career evolution that they'll never get back.

Am I arguing that loyalty and allegiance are a bad thing? It depends on what you're loyal to. Being loyal to a factory or a corporation with anonymous owners seems sort of silly. Being loyal to other people, people who trust you and want to help you grow— that's just common sense.

When the best people leave to join companies that let them zoom, runaway sets in. Those companies zoom ever faster, making them more fun, more stable and more profitable over time. But this process can't happen until individual employees realize that they do have a choice and take the power they have and put it to work at a place that will reward them (and develop them).

If you're not willing to zoom in your career, it's unfair to ask your company to zoom for you. As the foundation of your company (of any company), it's the posture of the people who work there that will determine how far and how fast that company goes. For more of my take on zooming, visit www.content.monster.com/zoom.

If You Want the Soup, Order the Soup

Jay's Sushi is a tiny counter inside the Korean vegetable market in my town. Just eight seats lined up along a wooden counter. Most people come for takeout, but the other day was sort of slow, so I sat down to eat.

While I was sitting there, people came up on either side of my seat to order takeout. I was busy eating my eel roll when a guy came up and ordered a miso soup. Just soup, nothing else. "How much is that?" he asked. "One dollar and sixty cents," said the smiling sushiman. Unfortunately, our heroic customer couldn't determine whether he was saying "sixty cents" or "sixteen cents" so he asked three more times. By now, all of us at the counter had memorized the cost of a bowl of miso at Jay's.

A few moments later, the woman sitting near me got her tray of sushi. She had ordered the deluxe, which costs twelve dollars for lunch. Salmon, tamago, the whole nine yards. As she admired the tray, she turned to the sushiman and said, "Does this come with miso?"

"Nope." He shook his head. "Do you want some?"

And to my amazement, the woman said no.

Now, either she wanted the soup or she didn't. She just dropped twelve bucks on lunch, she knew the soup was really cheap and if she wanted the soup, she could have asked for it, right? And that it "comes with" the meal doesn't mean she should eat it if she doesn't want it!

But then I realized something bigger was happening. Many of us react to what life brings us, but have a lot of trouble ordering something new off the à la carte list.

Most everyone is working harder than they ever dreamed of. There's no time for additional tasks, no time for new projects. Our

---

"Our to-do list is generated by other people, and we spend our day reacting and responding to external stimuli. It's easy to spend a day answering three hundred incoming e-mails without taking the time to initiate anything that matters to you."

---

to-do list is generated by other people, and we spend our day reacting and responding to external stimuli. It's easy to spend a day answering three hundred incoming e-mails without taking the time to initiate anything that matters to you.

Part of the challenge of zooming is that it requires internal initiative to start and run the system and then continued initiative to create new variations. This doesn't fit easily with the priority list of an already harried executive.

This lack of initiative happens most often with career and business strategy issues. One investor I know has a knack for backing companies that flame out dramatically, costing him money and creating all sorts of misery for all involved. He'll be the first to point out "I did everything I could" and then back it up with a litany of bad breaks, unfortunate outcomes and difficult choices he was faced with. Almost every one of these bad breaks was a result of an apparently unstoppable external event.

Phooey.

Will's problem is that he allows the problem to be defined by what's presented to him. He accepts the multiple-choice solutions that are offered and forgets that "none of the above" is a very valid response.

Companies are often criticized for being slow, being stuck and failing to capitalize on new opportunities. But companies are nothing but a collection of people. If you're stuck, perhaps it's because you're waiting to see what's on the menu. If you want the soup and they're not serving soup, perhaps you ought to find someone who is.

Starting Down the Road to the Zooming Organization

If I've been successful in persuading you to pursue runaway in all its forms by creating a zooming organization, and you work in a company that's filled with nonzoomers, the obvious question is: How do we transform this place?

Most new organizational and business ideas face this hurdle. The million-dollar question is: How do I get everyone in the company aligned, focused on the same tactics and willing to take risks in order to find success?

My answer may surprise you. *Don't.*

The idea of somehow pushing this technique onto the entire organization represents the same sort of management thinking that encourages us to believe we can control change. A company has to evolve into its position as a zooming organization.

Don't try to force the reactionaries to change. Don't spend hours cajoling the serfs to give up their bondage and become farmers, hunters and wizards. Yes, you should teach them how to think about these issues and understand these terms. Give them a chance to join you. But you can't force someone to embrace memetic evolution.

By focusing on the individual building blocks (people), you can create slightly larger blocks (teams, task forces, divisions) that

---

"How do I get everyone in the company aligned, focused on the same tactics and willing to take risks in order to find success?"

---

will start moving within the organization. Those blocks can achieve runaway when people who want to zoom start joining them.

If you try too hard to convert the entire organization, people will humor you and pretend to go along. And then they'll slow you down. They'll sandbag your new projects and hamstring your efforts to zoom.

Instead, make it voluntary. Find people who want to contribute, who read the right books and magazines, who are eager to make a difference. Offer them a chance to join a team that's going to drive one process or another. And then get out of the way. Leave the team alone. Give them real boundaries and real deadlines and a lot of freedom. They'll probably fail.

Reward them with public appreciation and maybe a raise. And then let them try something else.

Sooner or later, your teams will start to succeed. They'll discover a niche and learn to exploit it. They'll farm your existing systems and discover huge savings or new revenue.

Give them more kudos and another raise. And then accept volunteers for more teams. Soon, your zooming groups will be approaching runaway. More people who want to zoom will join the group, thus making it more likely it will zoom even faster.

When enough people have crossed the road to get to the other side, shut down the factories that are losing you money and move on. Extinction is a way of life. Shift happens. If people can zoom with you, you all win. Don't let the others hold you back.

True story: A colleague went to the CEO of a fast-growing public company. He asked him if he could set up a group of five people who would design the next generation of products the company desperately needed. They intended to move across the street, to a tiny low-rent office, and all five of them had volunteered to take a pay cut and more stock options as a way of demonstrating their confidence that they could invent something really worthwhile.

The CEO thought it over for a minute, and then said, "I can't let you guys do that. If I do, everyone else will want to do that too and we won't have anyone left to grind stuff out."

My friend doesn't work there anymore.

The Best Way to Stop Your Company from Zooming

If you really and truly don't want to evolve, it's pretty easy to stop it. Just set a standard for new initiatives that's impossible to hurdle. Let people bring you improvements and new ideas and then point out that they're not exceeding the hurdle. The wizards and hunters in your company will soon stop bothering you.

Then, make sure you give the serfs so much to do that there's no time for them to farm. "That's not the way we do things around here" is a great all-purpose mantra to reinforce your company's desire to keep things the way they are.

Hire a new executive but be sure that she absorbs all your memes, while being careful not to touch any of *hers*. The power of social exclusion is huge, so make it clear that learning the ropes is far more important than changing things—most people want to fit in, and direct feedback like that is usually sufficient.

Companies often forget that hiring is a two-way street. On one hand, you want talented serfs to carry out your policies. On the other, the sexual swapping of memes that comes from hiring smart people is the fastest, most efficient way to evolve your company—and the only way to get to runaway. Talented people don't want to go to work for a company that drains their initiative. And if you can't hire talented people, you're stuck.

My friend Zig Ziglar asks a great question: "Is there anything new you can do at work tomorrow that will demoralize your employees, anger your customers and depress your stock price?"

"You're not stuck if you don't want to be."

If your actions can do all those negative things, it's a safe bet that new actions on your part can do the opposite as well. You're not stuck if you don't want to be.

The Zooming Club

We need a secret handshake.

Really. We need a way to tell other people that we've decided to zoom, that our winning strategy is to evolve.

The easiest way to get to runaway is to signal to zoomers that your company is a great place to work—and then to keep that promise by doing everything you can to hire zoomers.

The easiest way for a zoomer to get ahead at a zooming organization is to signal her boss that she's emotionally committed and ready to invest the time to increase her zoomwidth.

There are some shortcuts. The first is the project-based approach I talked about earlier. Design teams and task forces that zoom and invite people to join. Your employees will self-select, especially after they see that employees that volunteer, advance.

What about external hires? How do we communicate to our future employees (or bosses) that we're looking for people who zoom? That's one of the reasons the vocabulary is so important. Once we can all use similar words to describe our goals, we save a huge amount of time and miscommunication.

In the meantime, here's a modest suggestion. In your help wanted ads, put a lowercase **z** in the bottom corner. Do the same with your résumé. The uninitiated won't notice it. The insiders, on the other hand, the ones in search of runaway, will see the **z** and be eager to talk to you about it. You can post your **z** résumé on monster.com.

And if that's too subtle, you can order your very own pin from my website at www.zoometry.com. Really. No joke. After all, how will we find out this doesn't work if we don't test it?

A Quick Lesson in Avoiding the Acquisition Trap

Many fast-growing companies fuel their growth by acquiring small companies. The goal, it seems, is not only to bring in smart people but to absorb the memes and expertise they've created. Since the acquired company evolved in isolation from the acquirer, it's likely that its memes are quite different. It has different ways of doing things and new ways of communicating—many of which are no doubt better (more fit) than those of the acquiring company.

In practice, though, it seems that some companies are satisfied to acquire only the assets. The sooner they can get rid of old management and their memes, the better. These companies respond

---

"Companies respond to the enthusiasm and input of the newly acquired team by shutting them out."

---

to the enthusiasm and input of the newly acquired team by shutting them out. In no time, the talented managers from the acquired company depart. Soon after that, the acquirer often realizes that the assets aren't worth as much as they thought—without the old management team's ability to evolve and tweak those assets, they waste away pretty quickly. Another failed acquisition.

The alternative is to put talented new managers in charge. No, they shouldn't run the entire company. But if a company was performing well enough to be worth acquiring, or an executive was talented enough to hire, why not let them change your company while they're still enthusiastic? By the time they've learned the ropes, they've also been indoctrinated into the way we do things around here.

The real irony is that time and again, a company will hire an individual, paying no premium at all, and ask him to head marketing, sales or manufacturing. But, after paying millions to acquire a company, a company rarely takes the stars of the acquired company and installs them in the very same executive positions that would have been available to them if they'd quit their job at the old company and come over individually.

Chapter 9

WHY IT WORKS NOW: FAST FEEDBACK AND CHEAP PROJECTS

> Technology enables zooming and evolution because it allows us to create fast and inexpensive projects, and lets us know right away if they're working.

Fast Feedback Loops

How long did it take Thomas Edison to find out if the movie projector would catch on?

First he had to invent the light bulb, then he had to invent and build the projectors, then seed the market with theaters and then hope that people would become directors and that directors would make movies (funded by investors!) and that people would pay to see them. It probably took him decades from the beginning to the end of that process.

When Procter & Gamble decided to enter the market for online cosmetics, they spent tens of millions of dollars and more than a year to build a factory that is like nothing else in the world. It can simultaneously mix and bottle and label hundreds of different variations of makeup at a time. And it creates each bottle specifically for one customer.

P&G assumed that their investment in Reflect.com would be a success (why bother spending that much if you expect to fail?) and built a state-of-the-art factory to support it.

Using Reflect.com's proprietary systems, a consumer could go to the site, answer a series of questions, have the data massaged by a "neural network" and end up with a choice from over three hundred thousand different customized products.

It's truly an amazing feat. Unfortunately, very few people have even been exposed to Reflect—about a quarter of a million people visit the site each month, with a tiny fraction of them actually buying the product. (To give you some perspective, the silly site amihotornot.com sees the same number of visitors every day). With funding from heavyweight investors, Reflect.com is in little danger of folding. But it took P&G several years and many millions of dollars to discover that the money being invested had quite a slow payback.

Got a great idea for a book? Well, it's going to take you two to six months to find a publisher and successfully sell it. Then another year from the day you sign the contract until the book hits the bookstores (if everything is moving smoothly). A few months after that and you'll know if the book is selling well. And a year after that you can expect your first royalty statement. All told, about two and a half years from beginning to end.

These long ramp-up delays and slow development cycles were state of the art when the competition was moving at a similar pace. Unfortunately, they now contribute to the failure of many projects.

When you expect success and organize entire systems around it, the delay in getting to market can actually diminish your chances of being successful. Worse, there's very little data to show that careful development combined with buy-in throughout the organization, combined with focus groups and the other trappings of big company product innovation increase your likelihood of success.

One of the main reasons behind the failure of intrapreneurship (new business development within companies) is that it takes too long. Too many people have to give too many approvals before anything gets done.

There's a meme we all learn as children. It's about persistence and the lonely voyage of the driven entrepreneur. One of the lessons good parents try to drive home with their kids involves, "If at

---

"When you expect success and organize entire systems around it, the delay in getting to market can actually diminish your chances of being successful."

---

first you don't succeed . . ." We try very hard to instill the sense of big visions and persistence in our coworkers and employees as well. It feels like a virtue.

In today's hypercompetitive world, though, in which the Red Queen is running rampant, it's not clear at all that this approach to the world is the most profitable way to run your business. The NASA space launch approach to new product development is certainly sexy, but is it the best way to bring something new to a competitive marketplace?

In fact, the opposite is largely true. The Palm was developed by one guy in a garage—and it continues to outsell Microsoft's heavily engineered solution. Hasbro didn't develop the Razor scooter, Maxwell House didn't launch Starbucks, IBM had nothing to do with Hotmail.

Low-cost, rapid product development works because it incorporates the power of evolution as well as using fast feedback loops.

The power of evolution? Yes, because the folks who brought us Starbucks and the Palm and the Razor didn't know they were going to succeed and they weren't famous before they started. They made small bets, and we only heard about them *after* they pulled it off. We only see the winning lottery tickets. What is left unsaid is that for every Steve Wozniak, there are a hundred or a thousand entrepreneurs who failed.

At any given moment, there are millions of people bashing at the gates of success, trying this and trying that. Most of the time they fail, just as most mutations in nature are failures. Every once in a while, though, there's a breakthrough and the rules change.

Notice that I'm not proposing that successful companies approve every hare-brained scheme and give employees carte blanche. To the contrary, excellent leaders help teach their employees to make smart choices. And great managers hold every person accountable for the promises they make. The faster a feedback system tells you you're failing, the better it's working. And the faster you kill a project that's failing, the better you're managing.

The most important factor that makes this possible is the idea of fast feedback loops. If you have to toil, like Edison, for ten or twenty or thirty years to find out if your innovation will matter, it's unlikely that you'll sign up for that sort of high-risk venture. But if you can start an internal project in January and find out if it's working by March, why not give it a shot?

Instead of building its fancy factory, P&G could have launched Reflect.com with the plan of filling the little bottles of cosmetics by hand. If the site was popular, *then* they could build the factory.

Fast feedback loops are the tactic that will enable the zooming corporation. Fast feedback loops use technology to turn data into information and to give us early warnings of successes (and failures).

There will always be room for the huge project, the ventures that require us to suspend disbelief and bet the ranch on an approach and an outcome, without knowing for certain if we're going to win until the very end. I'm arguing that for most of us, most of the time, the alternative is far smarter, more exciting and more likely to succeed—lots of small ventures, small efforts, small tests, that, when coupled with fast feedback systems, allow us to find out which changes to our winning strategy are most likely to be worth pursuing.

Note that there's a difference between a Test and a test. Tests that don't use real markets don't usually work. Focus groups or informal polling of the folks you run into in the hallway aren't really tests. Why? Because people who know you're doing a Test don't react the same way. Because people who are giving feedback on a Test are far more likely to be critical of really brave ideas, and far less likely to be critical of safe but stupid ideas. The power of fast feedback loops is that you can find out right now, from real people, whether your idea is worth pursuing.

As Thomas Edison said, "The real measure of success is the number of experiments that can be crowded into twenty-four hours."

The Power of the Obligating Question

The sales pro Zig Ziglar has popularized a technique he calls the obligating question. It's a way of turning a prospect's objections into real data.

When a salesperson is trying to close a sale and the prospect hesitates by objecting to some element of the product (often something the salesperson can't change, like the color or the price), the usual result is that salesperson walks back to headquarters, bellowing about how important it is to change the product.

Salespeople are often ignored by the home office, largely because in the past, when changes were made, the prospect didn't buy the thing anyway. Managing your product line based on the objections of people who aren't yet your customers is a dangerous policy.

The obligating question changes that. The salesperson asks, "If we are able to deliver x, y and z at the price you've discussed, are you prepared to go ahead and buy our product today?" At this point, the salesperson ought to bring out an order form.

You know what happens? Most of the time, the objections

"Managing your product line based on the objections of people who aren't yet your customers is a dangerous policy."

---

weren't real. The prospect wasn't ready to buy anyway, or there was some sort of hidden objection that this question brings out.

This is a smart thing to teach your salesforce, because they'll discover that much of the time the objections they're spending time on aren't the real ones, and the people they're calling on might not be able to buy your product in the first place!

But beyond the filtering effect of the obligating question, it separates wanting from needing. It quickly clarifies for all concerned what is nice to have versus what's going to actually lead to a market success. It's a real test.

Linux Is Cool—But It's Not What You Think

The Linux operating system is an alternative to Windows or the Mac. It offers several things that make it distinctive, though. First, it's free. Second, it's written by literally thousands of people, all of whom have worked on it for no pay. Third, it works really well— it's more stable than any of its competitors.

For obvious reasons, people have been fascinated with the Linux phenomenon. Here's this free operating system, possibly the most complicated piece of software in general use. It's written not by a team of options-rewarded, caffeine-stoked Microsoft engineers toiling away in secret, but by a very loosely knit amalgam of computer programmers all over the world.

Linux isn't the easiest operating system (here's a quotation from a web site on Linux: "An easy way to fire off a quick email is to use :*echo body | mail -s subject address* where body is the body of the email in quotation marks, subject is the subject of the email [also in quotation marks], and address is the email address . . .") but it is becoming more and more popular, especially for mission-critical applications.

While the open-source movement is indeed interesting, that's not why Linux is a model for a zooming organization. It's the fast feedback loops that make it work.

Somewhere in the world, someone is posting an update, a patch or an entirely new version of Linux every single hour of every single day. When a bug appears, or a new device driver is needed, programmers swarm around the problem and generate a solution in a matter of days or weeks.

At one level, this constantly updating, swarming approach to evolving an operating system is reassuring—the system is always getting better. But there is a danger. Like many forms of evolution, this incremental improvement can lead to dead ends. Just as a bunch of people building an igloo with no guidance are unlikely to have it come out properly, this approach can lead to less-than-elegant code. In fact, it can lead to really slow, kludgy stuff that no one wants to work with.

Enter a second level of evolution. While there's incremental farming going on all the time, there are other programmers taking a longer view. Because all the code is available publicly, anyone can rewrite whole sections of Linux. If this rewrite is smoother, faster or more efficient, it gets swapped in, replacing all the bad stuff. And the evolution continues.

Is Linux a business? Nope. Doesn't matter. Who cares that no money is changing hands? It doesn't change the dynamic nature of the process. They've figured out how fast feedback loops can take a cheap project and evolve it into a dominant player.

If thousands of programmers, working without pay with strangers in faroff lands, can create a product this functional and this complex, can't the same approach work for your company—using your advantages of full-time employees, organized communication and smart middle management?

Technology and Fast Feedback Loops

For a long time, Lotus Development spent money on all three parts of Lotus 1-2-3. They improved the spreadsheet, the database and the word processor. Then they did a study and discovered that 95 percent of their users never used anything but the spreadsheet.

Wouldn't it be useful to know how people are actually using your product, and more important, how they're *not* using it?

A range of new technologies is now being developed that will allow companies to have a far better idea of what actually happens after a product leaves the plant.

Microchips, for example, are now approaching a cost close to zero. This means that a manufacturer can embed chips into all of his products. He could know what percentage of the people reading *USA Today* ever bothered to open the sports pages. He could discover how many miles people put on a tire before they traded it in and bought a new one. He could monitor how many hours a week his new drill press is used at the average plant.

Better still, technology allows marketers to understand, in real time, what's working and what's not. Wal-Mart knows within minutes if a new product on display near the cash register is working or not, and can take action if it's not.

Using links with TiVo and other digital video recorders, a TV network can find out at exactly what moment people changed channels, allowing them to tweak a show the way QVC tweaks its airtime.

A company that makes tires, or bolts or ceiling panels can place chips in its products and discover precisely how long they last in actual use—and why and how they break.

A farmer can place sensors in various pieces of fruit and compute the best moment to harvest each tree in his grove.

Each of these innovations represents an insight—that knowing how something is used (really knowing, not guessing) can drive your company to success. Suddenly, the cost of knowing is dwarfed by the cost of *not* knowing.

I'll Know It When I See It—The Power of Prototypes

Michael Schrage has written persuasively on the benefits of prototyping. It's unlikely your boss can think as conceptually as you about the intricacies of your field, so showing is always better than telling.

New technologies make it fast and easy to build three-dimensional mock-ups of manufactured goods. You can build a web page in an hour. Design a book cover or a magazine ad in less than a day. Make a product *after* the ad proves that people want to buy it.

When the market is making choices based on look and feel (and assuming that the mechanics are perfect), then it makes sense for you to prototype based on look and feel now and add the mechanics later.

When Joseph Park was pitching Kozmo (the late, lamented, one-hour Internet delivery service) he used a simple prototype to make his point. At the beginning of the pitch to venture capitalists, Park would ask the people in the meeting their favorite flavor of ice cream. Then he'd type a few words into his laptop and go back to the presentation. Before the pitch was over, uniformed Kozmo delivery guys would show up with a pint of Ben & Jerry's for everyone in the room.

All the spreadsheets in the world couldn't take the place of that demonstration. He got his money. (He raised more than $200 million, actually.)

For some reason I don't understand, people are far quicker to give feedback on something that's already done, that's easy to hold and touch and work with. Using rapid prototyping techniques, companies like Boeing can save billions of dollars and years of time in developing new planes. It's much easier to show a potential buyer or a test pilot the Boeing prototype than it is to describe it.

Yet most firms resist prototypes, despite their ease of creation. Why, for example, would you program a complex web site until you had prototyped every single one of the important pages? It only takes a few days in Photoshop to fake it, and if you don't like what you see, now is the time to change it. Instead, most companies wait until they've invested a few million dollars (and a few months) before they start to criticize and tweak.

Most big software projects die because the specs are inadequately described, understood and embraced before the programming starts. An incredibly useful mechanism is to have a human being pretend to be the finished system. Then all the users of the system can throw the questions they'll be expecting the system to answer at the human instead. The process of "I'm sorry, I won't be able to answer that" will create a rapid evolutionary cycle that will save cash and heartburn.

There's almost no product or service made by a company that can't be made into a prototype before the factory is built or the people are hired. Yet most companies fail to even bother.

Schrage believes you can tell a lot about a company by the way it prototypes, and I agree. Most companies fail to prototype at all because it sends the signal that management is not omnipotent. Prototypes are, by definition, rough drafts, designed to be wrong, not right. The companies that are best at prototyping do many, many prototypes, as fast as possible, until they've whittled their

---

"There's almost no product or service made by a company that can't be made into a prototype before the factory is built or the people are hired. Yet most companies fail to even bother."

---

way to a product that's good enough to launch. Are rough drafts viewed as smart management in your shop?

Who has the right to make a prototype? Who has to approve it? How long does it take?

A Prototyping Pitfall

Companies create their future with their prototypes. By limiting what sorts of prototypes get built, and controlling who builds them and who interacts with them, management is already choosing its path. This is foolish. Evolution at this level is cheap and easy and incredibly leveraged.

At Kyocera, Gary Koerper had to beg, borrow and steal the thirty thousand dollars he needed to finish the final prototype of his team's new cell phone. If he hadn't broken corporate rules, that phone would never have been shipped. It became the fastest-selling phone of the year, all because one renegade manager broke the rules to finish something he believed in.

The command and control mindset wants to command and control who gets to make the prototypes and who gets to see them.

Yet the more individuals who work to create prototypes, the more likely it is that a positive mutation will occur.

Just as important, the presentation of prototypes needs to be constant and informal (and then, as they grow in importance,

---

"The danger, of course, is in falling in love with proto-typing and never actually shipping a product."

---

scheduled and formal). As the costs of feedback increase, you need to limit feedback. But Chrysler's model makes perfect sense—put your prototypes on public display! Over the last few years, beginning with the Dodge Viper, Chrysler has used concept cars as a marketing and development vehicle. The cool cars helped their brand and the feedback leads to real cars.

By parading concept cars in front of the public, Chrysler accomplishes four things:

1. It positions its brand as forward-thinking and cool.

2. It gets valuable feedback about what the public wants and doesn't want.

3. It signals future mates (the public and its dealers) that it's healthy.

4. It implements the Red Queen and changes the market-place for its competitors. It can wreak havoc in a market it's not even in just by displaying a car it may or may not make several years from now.

Apple Computer has used a similar approach. Externally demonstrating prototypes helps seed the market and, just as important, puts pressure on the internal groups to deal with the feedback (and evolve the concept) while they are actually working hard to make the thing.

The danger, of course, is in falling in love with prototyping and never actually shipping a product. Apple did this with their new operating system—prototypes were shown for more than a decade before it actually launched. That's why a hard stop and regularly scheduled (and publicly known) deadlines are so important.

Data Is Not Information—Keeping the Promise of IT

Over the last decade, companies have spent billions of dollars installing information technology (IT). The promise has been simple: IT creates connections. It connects employees to one another and it connects a company to its data.

A&P is in the middle of rebuilding its entire supermarket business around this idea. By installing more than $250 million worth of systems, it intends to track sales, inventory, yield and just about everything else worth measuring. Every A&P manager will be linked to headquarters by e-mail. It is rebuilding the company around the data.

And this IT project—like most IT projects—will fail unless the company learns to zoom. The data created by a large-scale IT installation quickly becomes a deluge. A music executive, for

---

"Why bother spending time to understand data if you're not going to do anything with the information once you find it?"

---

example, can track the sales of a new CD by day and by ZIP code. She can discover which formats are selling in which types of chain stores. And she can do this for all ten-thousand items in the catalog. What good is this much data?

Unless there's a bias toward fast feedback loops, the data is worthless. It never turns into information because it's just not worth the time. Why bother spending time to understand data if you're not going to do anything with the information once you find it?

If a company starts testing and measuring, the data on a test become extremely valuable. With the quick return on investment that comes from knowing the results of a quick and cheap test, employees will be motivated to extract real knowledge from the data. And once they do that, the huge investment in IT pays off.

Putting a Man on the Moon

The biggest objection to the zooming organization is that it makes it hard to launch the really big, really scary project. After all, if we'd been an opportunistic, evolving society in 1965, we would have scrapped the Apollo project and never gotten to the moon. We all know you don't build a rocket that goes halfway to the moon and then improve it. Instead, as we all know, you aim high and build a huge infrastructure and grab it all at once.

Big, scary projects require a mission control center. Note the word control. An essential lesson of evolution is that control is in short supply. You can control various parts of the process, but the outcome itself is never under your control.

In addition to mission control, big projects usually offer the organizer three other characteristics:

- All your eggs go in one basket. A few organizations might be able to launch simultaneous big projects, but more often than not, if it's that big, you're only going to do one at a time.

- You need lots of money, which means the cost of failure is very high.

- You need a long time frame and a stable environment. Without the stable environment, your long-term plans are useless.

My response to those who would criticize the zooming organization for forgoing the big, bold, hairy project is, "You're right." I'm not going to quibble about the fact that we did, in fact, build rockets that went halfway to the moon before we built the big one. While the Apollo project did evolve as it went, it also required a huge, focused investment on one and only one goal.

An evolving organization doesn't want to put all its eggs in one basket, because it's been demonstrated time and time again that organizations don't know how to pick the right basket. And the evolving organization resists spending a lot of money on one project for precisely the same reason. And finally, the evolving organization doesn't bother wishing for a stable environment, because everyone who zooms knows that that almost never happens.

That means that a nine-year-long project to put someone on the moon is not as likely to happen in an evolving organization. It means

---

"An evolving organization doesn't want to put all its eggs in one basket, because it's been demonstrated time and time again that organizations don't know how to pick the right basket."

---

that Apple's fifteen-year quest to build a new operating system would never occur at a company that zooms. If your goal is glory, the kind that comes in the guise of a fully formed, perfectly functional rollout, then this strategy is not for you. But a quick review of the return on investment of the Apollo-type corporate rollouts makes it clear: It may be glorious, but it's not the best way to succeed.

New technology makes it far easier to build cheap projects now. You can simulate Amazon's home page for a thousand dollars, while it might cost you $100 million to simulate Macy's store on Thirty-fourth Street in Manhattan. You can simulate a new line of sneakers or a new kind of Palm or a new weapons system for a tiny fraction of what it might have cost ten years ago.

Cheap projects mean that you get more chances to find the right project. The only people who don't benefit are companies obsessed with finding the right project before they launch anything. In the long run, those companies will always be defeated by the quick and the cheap.

A Broken Feedback Loop

Have you noticed that the folks at your local car dealership are treating you a little better when you come in for service? Well, maybe a little.

The reason is probably their increasing reliance on feedback loops. Many firms, including Ford and Volkswagen, call every one of their customers the evening after a service call. The caller goes through a script and asks a series of multiple-choice questions about your satisfaction with the service you just paid for. The good news is that this service is coordinated by the automaker, not the dealer, so there's a consistent approach and they can measure response across dealers.

It's pretty easy to see how this apparently harmless survey can radically change the way a dealer runs his entire company. If a dealer is treating customers poorly, the brand manager at the auto company cares a great deal, and can make the dealer's life miserable. As a result, the dealers are living and dying by the survey data. Too many low grades in "meet and greet" and the guy at the desk loses his job. Too many "my-problem-didn't-go-away" ratings and the entire staff of mechanics goes back to school for a refresher course.

So far, so good. The customer is more engaged and the dealership's service organization is always scrambling to evolve to stay on top of the ratings.

The problem lies, as it always does, in the execution. Let me tell you about Cityline Volkswagen in the Bronx, where we used to get our Beetle serviced.

At our first service, they made us stand outside in the rain for fifteen minutes, and then fixed only two of the three things we brought the car in for. The guy who helped us was charming and helpful, which counts for a lot, but still, when they called that night with the survey, I told them about the problems (bending over backward to point out the good stuff, too!).

When we brought the car back a few weeks later for them to install a new part, the same service manager was on duty. It turns out that Volkswagen doesn't just hand over the scores to the dealers, they also hand over each and every survey. The service manager saw us come in and said, "Hey, you're the guys who gave me a bad rating." He then proceeded to fire us as customers, explaining that he didn't want his rating hurt by people like us, and asked us to leave. He refused to install the part or to work on our car again.

I called the head of the dealership (hey, it was research for a book), but it was clear that the strategy was okay with him. His goal was for his dealership to collect a group of customers that either didn't bother to answer the survey or always gave high marks.

He'd figured out how to game the system. Which is what will happen to most systems if you let it. Volkswagen wanted Cityline to avoid getting low ratings, and Cityline decided the easiest way to accomplish this was to fire customers who gave them low ratings!

More common are situations in which the person who is in a position to give feedback doesn't gain by being constructive. In a corporate culture in which feedback is viewed as criticism and complaining, people aren't eager to get it, and may choose to avoid the source of the feedback. Obviously, that discourages people from offering it as well. **Hotwash** is one example of a feedback loop that forces the organization to distinguish between feedback and criticism and ensures that the loops don't break.

Implementing Hotwash

The army is famous for post-mortems. After a war game, the generals and officers get together and analyze everything that happened. And they do it that day, not a week or a month later. It's a version of a fast feedback loop, but with very special implications.

These hotwash sessions provide a breeding ground for new memes. By analyzing what just happened, you've bypassed the social prohibition against criticism by turning it into feedback. "Hey, we got trounced, let's find out why . . . and better yet, how to do better next time."

If it's part of the process, and it happens every time, it's impossible to be defensive. You can't take it as personal criticism because it's happening to everyone else.

The same sort of hotwash can work for your employees. Why not have the salesforce tape all of their phone calls (this is legal in most states). Burn the calls onto CDs and then have the salespeople pick their five favorites. Have groups of six or seven salespeople spend an hour a week, each playing each other their favorite calls. The exchange of memes will be significant. At the end of every month, distribute the best ten calls to every single one of your salespeople.

Why not do the same thing with boring PowerPoint presentations? At the end of every single presentation given inside your company, allot five minutes for the group to give feedback on the process and execution of the presentation itself. Within weeks, the quality of presentations (and the thinking that goes with them) will radically improve. By sanctioning the process of direct feedback, you're making it far more likely that evolution happens.

Most people will groan when they hear about an idea like this. It's not safe. It's not fun. It makes work less comfortable (at

---

"Most people will groan when they hear about an idea like this."

---

least for a while). I'd answer the groans by telling the story of the backpackers and the grizzly. In our competitive marketplace, if there's another company that's evolving by adopting hotwash, how will you compete if you don't?

A dreaded form of feedback is the annual review. Why waste time on them? Nine times out of ten, they're nonsense. The boss doesn't want to admit to waiting eleven months to point out that someone is doing a horrible job. The employee is defensive and on edge. Instead, why not do an "annual" review every day? If feedback is frequent, it's far easier to be constructive.

Obviously, experienced managers bristle at the idea of a daily hotwash. They could easily consider it micromanaging. And that's what it would be if it were done the way an annual review is done. Consider instead the idea of using hotwash as a fast feedback loop, one that's based on mutually agreed-upon metrics. Now, it's not a matter of opinion, or power. It's two smart people working together to make a metric go up from day to day.

One of the key traps of hotwash is the development of a mutual admiration society. It may be necessary to implement a rule that's the opposite of a brainstorming session: no positive feedback! Nature rarely delivers positive feedback to animals—if you're fit, you get fed, if not, you're extinct—and spending a lot of valuable time congratulating each other on our PowerPoints and sales calls is fun but not productive.

Please don't mistake these meetings for an endorsement of the sort of critical sniping that passes for feedback in companies today. Hotwash sessions work best when the feedback is about the performance, not the performer. They work even better when the feedback is substantial and measured, not vague opinion. And they work best of all when someone is keeping track of who's using the feedback to get better and who's just enjoying the opportunity to be critical of someone else.

Plan for Success . . . and Plan for Failure

In many organizations, you can't launch a new initiative until you've explored all the ramifications of success. "How will we ever build enough?" "What happens if everyone in the company wants one?" "Have you run all this by legal?"

If only one out of twenty (or thirty or a hundred) tests is successful, that means you're doing far more work than you need to. More important, it means that you're making it hard to launch new tests—which mean fewer tests will launch.

The key to planning for success is not investing in every contingency. It's knowing that you can pile on with short notice if you need to. Companies spend far too much time and money worrying about success.

We're afraid of having to turn away orders (and profits) because we were in too much of a hurry. Given how unlikely the success of any test is, though, I think it's better to take that risk than to explore every avenue in advance. The first day Federal Express flew, they delivered fewer than thirty packages. They had

> "Companies spend far too much time and money worrying about success."

fancy jets, a beautifully designed system and nothing to deliver. Perhaps the lead times on cargo jets is so long that the high initial expense was necessary. Even so, is your business as complex as that? I doubt it. Discover a likely winning strategy first. The logistics will follow.

Sound crazy? When investors were trying to determine whether CarsDirect.com had a future, they challenged the CEO to sell one car online. Just sell the car, then walk down the street, buy it from an authorized dealer and hand it to your customer. You didn't need a "factory" (in this case, a nationwide network of authorized dealerships) to test to see whether the offer to the consumer would work. In the first day, they sold four cars. It was enough. Now they knew they had to build the factory to support the idea.

Planning for failure is more difficult. Every plant you open, you're going to have to close or sell. Every employee you hire is going to leave or get fired. In a country where half of all marriages end in divorce—and yet few have a prenuptial agreement—it's not surprising that we don't like to plan for the likely outcome. We should.

When you take a job, how long do you wait before you start planning for your next job? Since you're going to leave sooner or later anyway, doesn't it make sense to start looking before you've decided to leave? To do otherwise creates a hurdle for you later— "is it *bad enough* that it's time to start looking for a job?" If you never have to ask that question, your winning strategy is less stuck.

Chapter 10

TACTICS FOR ACCELERATING EVOLUTION

Once a company understands the need to zoom, it can start to build tools that increase its ability to adapt to a changing environment.

Cherish the Charrette

Architects talk fondly about the exciting, crazy burst of energy they go through just before a presentation is due. You've got five or ten motivated, smart people, all working feverishly to finish something they've worked on for months. More often than not, the best thinking, the most important changes and the most innovative ideas come at the last minute. The process is so important and so common, they gave it a name. They call this a charrette.

Why are charrettes so productive? Because with deadline pressure and the collaboration that comes from knowing that "this is it," people are able to surrender their winning strategies. Even better, without time for approvals from everyone, things that are really clever manage to find their way in.

Can you create charrettes around your product and process? One way is to create deadlines where none existed. It's great that your team goes through a charrette once a year before the big trade show, but perhaps it's worth creating one or two other occasions each year where a similar deadline looms.

Charrettes aren't limited to architects, of course. Politicians go through one in the weeks leading up to an election. Students discover its power when their MBA study group only has a few days left until the presentation.

The power of the charrette is that when there's a hard stop on a project, people figure out how to prioritize their objections. Try this simple experiment: at your next decision-making meeting, bring an egg timer. Announce the decision that will be made unless the group agrees to a different decision before the timer runs out. After the stunned silence is over, you'll discover a very motivated group of people.

Are you still managing the process? Sure. You must set the timer. You need to make sure the right people and the right tools are in the room. And you need to have established an environment

---

"At your next decision-making meeting, bring an egg timer."

---

in which people can create without fear. Then get out of the way— the results will surprise you.

Animals Evolve on a Regular Schedule

Genes change when an organism is conceived. Memes, on the other hand, are in constant flux, meaning they appear to change more gradually. Paul McCartney's daughter represents a genetic shuffling of his genes with Linda's. In the same time it took for Paul to be born, find a mate and reproduce, he created thousands of songs, each a subtle (or dramatic) memetic step removed from the one that preceded it.

There are no markers for memetic regeneration. There's no natural time to give birth to a new idea. While some people are prolific (Paul McCartney didn't need an incentive to create more memes), others hold back, figuring that they can always launch that new idea tomorrow. You can dramatically increase the pace and impact of memetic change by creating artificial markers—call them birth moments. The launch of a new factory or a new web site or a new office is an occasion to implement a whole host of new memes at once.

Just as an organism must do all its genetic recombination at once in anticipation of an upcoming birth, your organization can be pushed to reorganize the contents of the meme pool in time for an upcoming marker.

Creating these opportunities and leveraging them is a positive step toward pushing the organization to zoom. McDonald's opens a new store every day. If they use these openings as opportunities to implement new systems, they can radically farm the old stores once they figure out what works in the old ones.

The flip side of this approach is the always-sliding deadline. If a new project launch can be extended ("We really want to get it right"), then the pace of memetic change will eventually grind to a halt. Someone needs to be pushing these things out the door, because until other people interact with them, you won't get substantial feedback to help you improve the next one.

If the cost of "launching" a new generation of product or service is quite small, your coworkers are going to be more likely to pull the trigger. And once they get into the habit of launching without stalling, the generations speed up.

Bring Back Model Years

Forty years ago, the new-car season was a big deal. People lined up outside the local Chevy dealership to take a look at the brand-new Corvette. There was a definite cycle in Detroit, with cars being designed, then engineered, then built, then sold, then cleared out—and then it started all over again.

Over time, the idea of Model Years has faded. Companies have realized that they can get more media and consumer attention by bringing cars out a little earlier. The market timing has blurred and now there's always something new.

What if a brand got back on a schedule that everyone was aware of? Perhaps it announced a new car design every month, for example. Imagine a standing GM ad at the back of *Car & Driver* magazine, featuring a different new model every month. This is a generational landmark for the engineers and the marketing people to strive for.

There's always something on every channel on TV. The producers never miss a deadline. The nightly news is always ready. They don't miss an episode of *E.R.* because they're still arguing about the script. Producers know that missing an episode means the end of their career. They also know, though, that an interesting broadcast that isn't a total winner isn't the end of the world.

Start introducing new ideas on a regular schedule.

Alternate the Teams that Work on New Models

One problem with **birthing moments** is that there's a temptation to place them quite close together. If one car model a year is good, two must be better. But once they take place too frequently, the team working on the introductions will no longer view them as charrette-worthy birthing moments. Instead, they'll view it as a constant process. The charrette will disappear. The emergencies will go away and you'll be back to where you started. The trick is finding a balance between constant evolution and constant grind.

Microsoft has a great solution. They have two different teams working on operating systems, each releasing a new system every two years. Thus, the folks who created Windows 98 are not the people who built Windows NT.

This system offers a wide range of advantages. First, there's a temptation (encouraged by management) for one team to steal the best of the other's ideas. But there isn't a matching desire to steal the bad stuff! Thus, no one has to cover his ass by pretending some piece of code created by a senior engineer on the other team is any good. They can ignore that and just take what works.

Even better, the alternating system allows Microsoft to compete against anyone who'd be brave enough to take them on in this field. By bringing out a full-blown new operating system every

---

"Remember, picking the lottery numbers doesn't increase your chances of winning the lotto—buying more tickets does."

---

twelve months, they're able to upgrade more often than any traditional company could (Linux is an exception because it's not traditional) and thus make this niche unattractive to competitors.

Furthering that advantage, team A can take the public feedback on team B's work and put it to use right away, while team B has to wait an extra year before they can use that feedback. Without being defensive (it's not their code) the folks on team A can use the constructive feedback to evolve their work before the public even sees it.

Generally, one design team handles one product. They do this for Corvettes and Palms and Macintoshes and Starbucks stores and Air Jordan sneakers. By alternating the teams, the internal competition and overlapping development cycles could accelerate the design and feedback process on all of these products. Remember, picking the lottery numbers doesn't increase your chances of winning the lotto—buying more tickets does.

Better Beats Perfect

Most organizations hesitate to implement an improvement because they are waiting for something better.

Isaac Asimov wrote a new book every six weeks. Some of the books were classics, some were merely good. All of them, however, were far better than the books J. D. Salinger never wrote.

In a competitive marketplace, there's no such thing as perfect. By the time you develop perfect, your competition will have changed the landscape so much that your product won't even be good any more.

Over and over again, Microsoft has demonstrated that shipping a mediocre product but following it up with a much-improved (and evolved) version will always defeat a competitor who's still busy working on their first version. In a world that's networked, it's far easier to fix after launch than it used to be.

It's about more than computers. Bob Dylan has produced more than fifty records, Chiat Day has launched thousands of ad campaigns and Procter & Gamble has more than a dozen varieties of Ivory.

When you embrace good instead of perfect, it makes your company faster. Why? Because you're willing to make decisions based on less-than-complete information. Because people are willing to give you more chances to fail. Because you're absolved of the responsibility of always being right.

If you're stuck waiting for something to be perfect, it's very hard to get the feedback you need to make it better.

Slow Down Is Not the Opposite of Hurry Up

In times of crisis, when *60 Minutes* is at the door or bankruptcy is around the corner, many businesses are able to hurry up and make dramatic changes. They rip and tear and aggressively undo all they've done while they scurry to build something new. All too often, these last-minute changes are too little, too late.

Evolution doesn't work this way. As long as there is competition (and there's always competition), species are evolving, testing new survival and adaptive strategies and trying to find a competitive edge. Over time, those tests (combined with inheritance) can add up to a significant advantage for the species.

A business that's not facing a life-or-death crisis doesn't need to slow down. It needs to hurry in a very different way. Hurry to evolve. Hurry to test.

Change is not a spigot to be turned on in an emergency and then sit blissfully turned off the rest of the time. It's a constant process, a tool for beating the competition.

When we were on the farm, there was a natural limit to how much anyone could work. More hours didn't produce more corn. More sharecroppers didn't generate more income. There was a limit to labor, and it was based on the yield of the land.

Factories changed that. In a factory, the more you work, the more you get. Even better, the more your employees work, the

---

"Change is not a spigot to be turned on in an emergency and then sit blissfully turned off the rest of the time. It's a constant process, a tool for beating the competition."

---

more you get. Industrialists demanded more employees and more time from each of them because it led to more profits for the owners of the factory. Employees fought back, unionized and won the forty-hour workweek.

Stock options and the new economy doomed the forty-hour week. Most of us are working too hard. We're not getting enough done, but we're working too many hours. White-collar employees (and part owners) find it easy to suspend our objections to over-time. It's macho to work all the time. Face time and all-nighters appear to be the best ways to succeed. Yet, it's not clear to me that companies with employees who work all the time outperform those that don't. Certainly, there's little correlation between productivity and hours worked, complexity of work and hours worked or stock value and hours worked.

We are no longer in the business of making stuff. Stuff is not where the big profits come from or the successful winning strategies are built. We make decisions instead of widgets. And working long hours doesn't help your company make more decisions, and it doesn't help your company make better decisions.

In fact, I think the long hours are an excuse for avoiding decisions, and a way for nervous managers to restore the factory-centric view of work. Companies with smart people who work less but make better decisions are going to win every time.

And the first decision smart companies make is: when to change. If you work for a company that is too busy acting like a factory, it will never find time to evolve. But if it has slack built in (the slack needed to make good decisions), then abandoning today's winning strategy and embracing tomorrow's is just good business, not a crisis.

How hard should you work? If you're working too hard to take the time to change, you've just answered the question, haven't you? We make decisions, not stuff.

What to Do if Your People Get Stuck

How can you motivate a group of successful people to give up their point of view before it's too late? In many cases, you can't. They're too fat, too happy, too sure that they know how to do it and that there are no other right answers. These employees are at an evolutionary dead end, and their mDNA has calcified. They want to be serfs, so let them.

Create teams of naive novices, people who bring a beginner's mind to a problem. They haven't figured out all the ways that are impossible, so they're far more likely to come up with solutions that are bad—and then motivated enough to evolve those solutions into ones that work.

PayPal, the online payment system that is a true Internet success story, was not started by American Express. This fascinates me because it's the perfect product for them to be running. And you've got to believe that Amex had hundreds of people working on new Internet-related projects when PayPal pulled the rug out from under them.

What happened? The folks at American Express were busy trying to make tiny adjustments to defend a long-running winning strategy. Amex knows how to make money in a certain way, and PayPal rejects many of these techniques. Amex has a culture of stability, and no one there wants to do more than tweak the winning strategy. The sort of stretch that PayPal brings to the party is out of the question. Because PayPal's approach is so different (compared to the changes Amex was comfortable with), the powers that be at Amex couldn't even begin to riff on it.

Is PayPal an incremental change on the Amex winning strategy? Most outsiders would agree that it is. But from the point of view of Amex management, it's as different as it would be if they sold ice cream.

Since PayPal's launch just about two years ago, they've signed up nine million members (with credit cards or checking accounts on file) and they're growing at almost a million members a month. During that period of time, they've changed their interface frequently, evolved from a primitive system to one that gets smoother and easier to use all the time. They're farming the process, taking their initial mutation and making it better and better.

So what's a big company to do? The first thing is to take the naysayers out of the loop. There was no one at PayPal who needed to be convinced before they were allowed to launch the product. Every person at the company was there because they already *believed*. Every time a big company holds a meeting designed to get buy-in or to persuade the reactionaries, that company is wasting time its smarter competitors are not wasting.

Putting the revolutionaries in their own building with real deadlines and frequent prototypes is a smart strategy. Protecting

---

"Take the naysayers out of the loop."

---

them from senior managers with lots of experience who can tell them what can't possibly work is smarter still.

One Thing Worth Stealing from the Supermarket

Milk comes with an expiration date. Dairies know that if they leave it on the shelf forever, it's going to spoil and someone will get sick.

The same thing is true at your company. A decision gets made and it's far easier to live with it forever than it is to get a quorum together to undo that decision months or years later.

Instead of making decisions forever, why not figure out which sorts of policies and tactics ought to expire? That is a fine brochure, for example, but I want a new one to replace it within eighteen months. Or this distribution partner is perfect for us, but we need to have three others in place by the end of the year.

Once you set an expiration date, stick with it. Either put the date right on the object (this machine to be sold for scrap on 1/3/05) or keep a running file, easily accessible, of when something needs to be discarded. If you know something isn't forever, it makes it easier to start something new. Getting married should be a big deal—launching something at work should not. Note that an expiration date is not a deadline. It's the date there's going to be a vacuum—and your company will just have to substitute the next-best available strategy.

There are two kinds of expiration. The first and more modest approach is merely to have a date on which you will reconsider a policy or a strategy. The second, which leads to far more evolutionary activity, is to promise to discard it and require the company to come up with something better. This sounds radical (and wasteful), but there are plenty of industries that stick with this (fashion, publishing, cars). The fact is that these industries evolve certain parts of their businesses far faster than most.

Why does *The New York Times* still run the stock tables? Does anyone read them anymore? I mean, if you really care what AOL stock is worth, the Internet is faster and easier to use and has bigger type. They certainly don't run them because they make a profit—there are essentially no ads on those pages.

The answer is that it's easier to keep running the tables than to deal with all the internal meetings. And it's easier to keep running the tables than to deal with the one thousand angry letters from reactionary readers who miss them.

That momentum (some would call it laziness) is costing the *Times* millions of dollars a year in wasted paper, and even worse, keeping them from inventing something else to put on those pages that might make a profit! If they expired, though, it might be a very different story.

The Eternal Web Page

Over the last five years, corporations have put up more than three billion (with a b) web pages. And most of the web pages will stay up, untouched and unmeasured, until we run out of electricity.

There's nothing easier to test and evolve than a web page. The systems for tracking and changing pages are cheap or free, and there's

---

"If anything needs an expiration date, it's your web site."

---

no specialized knowledge necessary to figure out that this layout did better than that layout. Yet almost no company evolves its pages.

The average web site stays up for forty-four days before it is taken down or altered. For all intents and purposes, that's forever. A web page ought to stay up for a day, maybe two.

The web is nothing but a direct-marketing medium, and every page is nothing but an offer page. No self-respecting direct marketer would leave a page untested and untouched for forty-four days. If anything needs an expiration date, it's your web site.

Imagine that a company is paying fifty cents, on average, in marketing costs to get one person to one web page one time. If ten thousand people go to that page a day, it's costing them five thousand dollars.

Now, imagine that 20 percent of the people who visit that page go to the next page, and 3 percent of those people become customers, with a lifetime value to the company of eighty dollars.

A quick look at the math demonstrates that every day, this process is generating about thirty new customers at a net loss of two hundred dollars a day.

If the firm started testing and measuring and evolving those two pages, it might be able to get the yield of the first page to 40 percent and the second page up to 5 percent. Now the math tells a different story. The net profit is now eleven thousand dollars a day. Even without increased marketing, these two pages might be able to contribute four million dollars a year in new profits.

The total cost of the tweaking: an hour a day of someone's time for a month.

Everybody Brainstorms

Despite their simplicity, nearly every **brainstorming** session goes wrong. Rather than allowing a million new memes to sprout, brainstorming sessions almost invariably turn into meetings at which the winning strategy is enforced and reinforced.

If you've ever said, "That's not the way we do things around here," during a brainstorming session, you're guilty. Also on my hit list is, "Well, I can save you some time and tell you that that's not possible."

The goal of a brainstorming session (and there are plenty of books that can give you all the implementation details) is to free the room from the constraints of the winning strategy and let new memes float around. There's plenty of time to shoot them down later. When you feel free to say something foolish, you're far more

---

"There's plenty of time to shoot them down later."

---

likely to say something profound. Why? Because your internal censors shut down, and freeing up those ideas that you've always been afraid to say out loud.

In addition to being run incorrectly, the sessions often involve precisely the wrong people. Instead of inviting just the marketing honchos to a marketing brainstorming meeting, invite some folks from the salesforce, the factory floor, your gym and even someone who used to work for the competition.

These naive beginners are far more likely to stretch the boundaries of what you're considering. And by seeding your thoughts with unfit memes, these folks are giving you the building blocks you need to build something better.

The Suggestion Box Is Not Dead

The factory-centric model of viewing employees as cogs in a wheel has led to a long tradition of bosses ignoring the workers. As long as they show up on time and press the right buttons, many companies are satisfied. Yet it's the workers who know the best ways to farm the systems you've got in place. Eastman Kodak installed the first suggestion box in 1898, but for over a hundred years companies have used them as a palliative, not an engine for change.

At the Bic pen factory, improvements from the floor are a way of life. Weekly meetings review every single suggestion, and the employees have become so involved that last year 85 percent of the workers made at least one suggestion, with about three thousand coming in over the course of the year.

The suggestions themselves are not the point, though. Bic doesn't pay very well (one hundred dollars for the best suggestion of the month), so this huge response rate isn't for the money. The reason it works is that it's created an environment where all employees are taught to continually farm all of their systems. "When I came to Bic twenty years ago, the thinking was, 'I just have to press these buttons; I have engineers to do the thinking for me,'" one employee said. Now, people think when they come to work.

Procter & Gamble has taken the process even further. It built a web site for suggestions (fast feedback!) and then added a database. Now, someone submitting a suggestion sees all the other suggestions that have been made that are similar. The number of entries in the database just hit ten thousand. By making connections between these memes, P&G makes it far more likely that the suggestions that are implemented are effective.

The good news about the site is that the CEO, John Pepper, had the bright idea of opening it up from the small R&D department to the whole company. By using the worldwide power of the web, he's spread this idea far and wide. The bad news is that it's a far less powerful force for cultural change than the simple Bic meeting.

Bic has changed the posture of its workforce. By encouraging them to look for improvements, and reinforcing this behavior with weekly meetings, at which peers and supervisors cheer on those who are improving the workplace, Bic has sent a powerful message. P&G on the other hand is taking a far more clinical approach. While it may get more mileage out of the suggestions, it's not clear that they're treating the workforce differently.

Take the Dumpster Test

One of the suggestions that came from Bic's farmers was about their Dumpster. It turns out that twice a week, a carting company picked up their trash—even though the Dumpster was never more than half full. By switching to pickup once a week, the company saved thousands of dollars.

So here's the question: If there were a similar situation at your company, how many people would try to save the money? How would they go about it? Would those people be seen by all the people they interacted with as troublemakers or oddballs?

This all goes back to posture. The idea of improving your systems to find ways to evolve is obvious, but it's not natural. The guy in operations who's in charge of trash pickup might resent the outsider making the suggestion. "Mind your own business" didn't become a cliché for no good reason, after all.

Instead of having the plant manager spend a lot of time trying to figure out how to save money on trash pickup, it makes more sense to spend that time changing the culture, so that hundreds of people start worrying about trash pickup.

Living with Broken Windows

In *The Tipping Point*, Malcolm Gladwell writes about the precipitous decline in crime in certain parts of New York City. He points out that by fixing broken windows and cleaning up graffiti, the police department created a new atmosphere. Studies have shown that when small vandalism isn't present, the rates of murder and robbery go down.

The reason seems pretty simple—if the neighborhood feels well cared for, it's harder to take actions that are against the law. If, on the other hand, you're living in the Wild West or a crumbling slum, all bets are off.

So what does this have to do with Verizon?

If you live in the northeastern United States, you've probably had to call Verizon about your phone service. When you do, you're greeted with a voice processing system that asks a number of questions and then says, "Please type in your phone number." So you type in the ten digits and then wait on hold for a while.

The next part of the process amazes me. Every single time I've been connected to someone over the last three years (perhaps twenty incidents), the operator says, "What's your phone number?" And then I say, "You mean the phone number the system just asked me to type in?"

At this point, the operator heaves a deep sigh, tells me that everyone says that and explains that the system doesn't work. (Remember, this is the PHONE company!)

Over the years, a few brave phone operators have surely forwarded this common source of frustration to the powers that be. And over the years, the engineers have always had something better to do than fix a system that annoys tens of thousands of people every day. That's a prioritization decision that I can't make for them.

But I can tell you that Verizon is making it very clear to the people who answer the phones (the folks who deal with their customers) that improving systems is not part of their job.

Ask ten Verizon operators to go to a brainstorming session about how to improve customer service and I'm sure you'll come up with a thousand great ideas. And I'm just as sure that Verizon doesn't zoom enough to have sessions like this. By leaving broken windows on their voice mail, they remind their operators and their customers of this every day.

Let's Test It!

In 1997, my company was doing a mailing to two hundred thousand of our users. Our goal was to get as many people as possible to open the e-mail as a first step toward getting them to actually respond.

One of the marketers in our brain trust came up with the

"How many Microsoft engineers does it take to change a light bulb?"

wacky idea of using the following subject line in the e-mail: How many Microsoft engineers does it take to change a light bulb?

In most companies, a suggestion like this would get you thrown out the door. But we had a farming mindset, so my response was very different. I said, "Hey, let's test it." And so we sent it to ten thousand of the two hundred thousand people who got the mail.

Guess what? The Microsoft e-mail got *twice* the response rate of the other one. We discovered that without using focus groups or hiring expensive consulting firms. We did it through testing.

Macy's can't overhaul the first floor of their store in New York City without spending millions of dollars and then taking a huge revenue hit if they're wrong. Amazon, on the other hand, can change things on their home page in an hour and revert to the original in five minutes if they guessed wrong.

This seems like an easy and obvious strategy for dot-com companies. Now, though, thanks to a wide range of technological innovations, just about any job held by a serf can be approached with the posture of a farmer instead.

Do the cashiers at McDonald's see a running total of how many of their customers ordered dessert? What if they did? What if they could see, right there on the cash register, what percentage of their customers were buying an apple pie compared to the other cashiers in the store or compared to the other stores in that region?

Given a goal, "sell 20 percent more apple pies," and a reward, "and win a free bike," as well as the freedom to improvise, my bet is that they could make the number soar. Imagine ten thousand cash register folks at McDonald's, all trying various smiles, come-ons and invitations just so they could win a bike. Sounds a lot like natural selection to me.

It gets even better. Once McDonald's discovers a few cashiers who seem to have a knack for this sort of thing, they can videotape them and share that approach with the other cashiers. A farming posture turns these ten thousand serfs into farmers, or at the very least, farmer's apprentices.

This change in mindset, a new posture, is a fundamental building block in creating a zooming organization. I pitched an idea to someone I know in publishing. Instead of saying, "How much will it cost to find out if it works, how long will it take and how much damage will be done if we're wrong?" she said, "That will never work and the publisher will never go for it." End of discussion. She's a serf, not a farmer. Her old rules have gotten her this far and she's in no hurry to discover better ones.

In my work with AOL, it seemed to me that they never learned how to farm. They were so busy with hunting and wizardry that they never bothered to test. For example, at one point AOL was one of the largest sellers of computer books in the world. In addition to selling computer books online, AOL operators would call users at home (during dinner) and sell them packages of books by phone.

Thinking like a direct marketer, the obvious thing to do was to test every possible script (for the phone) and online presentation that made sense. Along those lines, stealing a technique from the great

---

"Her old rules have gotten her this far and she's in no hurry to discover better ones."

---

direct marketers of our time, the other smart strategy was to test books before you wrote them. Call a thousand people or run a thousand online ads and see if the book you had in mind was going to sell. If it did, hurry up and write it. If not, go on to the next idea.

While the economics of this idea are obvious, AOL staffers didn't think like farmers. They wrote the books first and sold them later.

Should There Be a Statute of Limitations on mDNA?

I'm not sure, but I think that in all the *Star Trek* episodes, no one ever celebrated a birthday. If they did, I'd bet money that they sang that stupid *Happy Birthday* song. More of a dirge than a chant of celebration, *Happy Birthday* is the official song of birthdays throughout the country. Going on a hundred years, it is firmly entrenched as the standard. I don't think I've ever been to a birthday party at which the song wasn't sung.

And it doesn't show any sign of going away.

Why take the risk? Why go to all the trouble of running a birthday party, only to disappoint the guest of honor by not singing the song? There's little doubt that we could come up with a better song. A funnier song. More joyous. More interesting. But it's extremely unlikely that with *Happy Birthday* stuck in the system we're going to find many talented songwriters eager to take up the challenge.

The same thing is probably true in your company.

There are rituals and winning strategies that no one has the guts to question, never mind replace. Go to Yahoo.com and click on the biggest logo on the page (the Yahoo! logo). For more than five years,

---

"Why go to all the trouble of running a birthday party, only to disappoint the guest of honor by not singing the song?"

---

that logo has been there, dominating the page, and it gets clicked on at least once (sooner or later) by every single person who visits.

Yet clicking on the logo on Yahoo!'s home page does precisely nothing.

Think of all the things you could do with that link. The biggest logo on the most popular page on the entire Net. Surely there are dozens of ways to profitably put that real estate to work. Instead of just leaving it there, why doesn't Yahoo! challenge its clients to come up with interesting uses for the link? And then test them, one by one, on portions of the population until something really works.

Or consider the United Way. The United Way grew to one of the largest charities in the world on the strength of a unique winning strategy: payroll deduction. By selling just one person at a big company, the United Way was able to reach hundreds of thousands of donors, each of whom could make small donations with every paycheck. It's brilliant!

Alas, with the fragmenting of the workforce, those big companies don't account for as many paychecks as they used to. More and more people are working for small companies or as freelancers. Suddenly, United Way's winning fundraising strategy isn't as effective as it once was.

Because the United Way stopped searching for new winning strategies when this one took off, the decline in expected donations that they're facing today is particularly painful. Perhaps they could have taken a different approach. If they had launched a significant new attempt at fundraising in each of their local chapters every year, at the end of twenty years they'd have tried more than three thousand new fundraising efforts. That constant, consistent effort to replace the current winning strategy would have turned up dozens of winners, ensuring stable growth for the charity. Instead, people saw payroll deduction as their *Happy Birthday* song—stuck forever.

Does Chaos Outside Mean Chaos Inside?

It may appear that the best way to deal with the turbulence of change is to encourage your company to enter a state of anarchy. I don't believe that's true. While there is no invisible hand guiding nature away from dead ends (like the platypus), it's pretty clear that intelligent leadership is the critical distinction between a company that zooms to success and one that just fades away.

There are four ways to keep an evolving company from devolving into a maddening mass of dumb projects while still permitting the easy adaptation of successful test results.

First, keep your projects cheap. Experiments that lead to natural selection or mutation are essential, but cheap experiments can

---

"Intelligent leadership is the critical distinction between a company that zooms to success and one that just fades away."

---

give you almost as much data as expensive ones. Cheap, by the way, also means fast. If there's a fast, cheap way to discover a better winning strategy, do it!

Eternal vigilance is required to keep fearful employees from building all sorts of guarantees and assurances into their experiments. If you're going to fail, fail quickly and cheaply. Don't let people build task forces and contingency plans and buffers around their efforts. Shoot first, ask questions later.

Second, hold people accountable. Not the sort of life-and-death accountability that passes for accountability at most companies. That sort of proposition all but guarantees that only an idiot would volunteer to test something—it's a sure way to lose your job. The kind of accountability you need is quick and direct. If someone promises a test will be done by Thursday, ask him on Thursday for the results. If they're a week behind on a two-week test, cancel it. Nature isn't kind and neither are evolving companies.

Third, you still need to lead. Successful companies defeat unsuccessful companies when a smart boss makes smart choices. No, this isn't genetics. Someone is in charge, at some level, and it's you. You decide which projects to authorize, which resources to allocate, which company to work for, what job to do.

Fourth, owners make better decisions. When Hard Manufacturing gave its factory workers a piece of the profits, a hundred experiments spontaneously occurred. Almost all of them were smart, and most of them translated into successful improvements in efficiency.

You cannot abdicate all decision-making to the market. I don't believe that management can dictate the future by fiat, but I

"We make bets every day, and making many bets is smart."

---

also know that having no position at all is an abdication of your responsibility. We make bets every day, and making many bets is smart. Making successful bets is brilliant.

Focus Is No Longer Sufficient

If you want to open a champagne bottle, it won't do to give the cork a little tug, declare that the test was a failure and then move on to the next champagne bottle. At this rate, you'll never get one open.

In business, as in champagne bottles, intense effort by a focused individual (or team) can make a huge difference. A gene is relentless in its efforts to spread. As far as that gene is concerned, nothing else is nearly as important as spreading. It's this sort of selfishness that allows the gene to thrive. The same is true of any effort in business. The ones most likely to succeed are the result of relentless, focused effort to the exclusion of just about everything else. If someone is more focused and more persistent, he is likely to triumph.

How then to rationalize the dictate that zooming organizations believe in frequent, cheap projects? Surely those organizations will end up losing to an obsessed competitor who will bet everything on launching this product or defending that market?

In the abstract, this is absolutely correct. Real breakthroughs often require a combination of investment and persistence. In practice, however, this is not what most traditional companies do.

They don't focus. They don't invest intelligently. Instead, they overinvest as a perceived insurance policy against failure. Focus involves peripheral vision. Focus implies an obsession with a goal, but flexibility about the means to get there. Excluding alternatives, on the other hand, allows a company to wear blinders and ignore all input it doesn't like.

When I first visited Jake Weinbaum and his team at Disney's online venture, I was stunned. It was around 1997, early days online, and they were supremely confident. Their huge offices were being wired with hundreds of thousands of feet of color-coded networking cables. There were T1 lines and fancy cubicles and a beautiful office building. I remember thinking at the time,

---

"Real breakthroughs often require a combination of investment and persistence. In practice, however, this is not what most traditional companies do."

"This is a lot of money to spend on a totally unproven venture." In retrospect, they probably would have been better off using the same money to seed a dozen or more businesses with different approaches to the Internet. Disney invested enough, but they "focused" too much and their money was wasted.

Our bias as managers is to try to find insurance. The idea of launching projects that we fully expect to fail (we just don't know *which* are going to fail) is anathema to the Harvard Business School way of thinking. So when I propose that a company evolve with a portfolio approach, I don't think you will go overboard and lose focus. The instinct to stick to the knitting is just too strong for it to be abandoned altogether.

The rule of thumb is to invest as little time and money as necessary—not a penny less. And of course, not a penny more. Put every dollar and person necessary on a project . . . and then use the rest to staff a project that takes a very different view of the world. The art involved in this process comes when management has to decide how much is enough to invest in a given effort.

Focusing on an effort does not mean your company can't focus on a competing effort as well. That, in fact, is the difference between companies and individuals. A company can focus on two things at once.

Bringing It All Together: Decision Time at Environmental Defense

To give you a glimpse of how a company that "gets it" can put zooming and evolutionary thinking into action, I've chosen an organization that's very different from yours, facing different decisions and a very different environment. The reason is simple: I don't want the details to get in the way of the simple logic that drives the decision.

Unlike most nonprofit organizations, Environmental Defense (formerly the Environmental Defense Fund) is not stuck in a winning strategy.

Founded about thirty years ago over a fight to ban DDT (which they won), this aggressive organization has been at the forefront of new ideas in the battle to save our environment. Most recently, they've been a standout in the use of the Internet to raise money and coordinate activists. Older, larger, more established nonprofits have either ignored the potential of the Net or strangled innovation with endless meetings and compromises.

To date, Environmental Defense has launched a range of sites. They include:

www.actionnetwork.org

This is an online activism hub. Environmental Defense signs up users and then sends e-mails like this one:

ACTION NETWORK ALERT—

Dear John Doe,

As you know, two weeks ago President Bush walked away from a campaign promise to lower carbon pollution from big power plants. In that announcement, he also questioned the basic science on global warming, a point of view far outside the mainstream of science. You joined with over 12,000 other Action Network members to register your concerns about this bad decision.

We're sorry to report that today he went even further.

The Bush administration has just announced that it will walk away from the only international effort to deal with global warming—the Kyoto Protocol. This agreement represents the world coming together to take initial steps toward limiting carbon pollution. It is currently the world's best hope to limit the effects of global warming. The United States signed this agreement in 1997 and has been hard at work negotiating its implementation in order to make it practical and workable. President Bush's decision abrogates a US commitment to the rest of the world, and could throw away hard won international progress on this crucial issue.

BUT WE ARE NOT GIVING UP. THE ISSUE IS TOO IMPORTANT!

You stood with us two weeks ago to urge the President to take global warming seriously. Now we must redouble our efforts. The Administration must begin to understand that these decisions are not only bad policy, they are bad politics as well. They must begin to understand that the public does not and will not support these kinds of decisions. Please join with us again to make the point to the President: these decisions cannot stand.

Sixty percent of the activists who received this letter responded and took action. Given that this is more than *fifty times* the response you'd expect from direct mail, it's no wonder that the web is changing the way Environmental Defense does business.

www.formyworld.com/

This is a site for the nonenvironmentalist. Its primary goal is to get nonactivists to make a behavior change and become more environmentally friendly. Also, over time, Environmental Defense wants to motivate people to take action and in the process join the for my world action network.

www.scorecard.org/

This site makes it easy to look up environmental facts and hazards about your neighborhood. For example, I discovered that the county where I live has cancer hazards one hundred times greater than those defined by the Clean Air Act.

Given the rapid start that Environmental Defense has had online, it's no surprise that they're excited about the potential for using this medium to grow their "business." Without significant investment or a top-down directive, the organization has evolved to use the medium in a productive way—one that shames many of their "competitors."

Through a mutual friend, the executives at Environmental Defense asked my advice. They had tested several sites and learned from the fast feedback loops that they'd set up. They now wanted to know how to spend some serious money and really pile on to this new winning strategy.

"Seth," they wanted to know, "which marketing companies should we use? Which developers? If we can get the board to approve a significant investment, what should we build?" This is a classic management question, and a specific one that I get asked all the time.

This time, though, a light went on for me. I drew a picture:

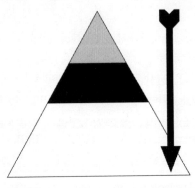

"Most companies want to manage from the top down. In this case, for example, Environmental Defense wants to figure out the 'right' answer, organize for it, spend a lot on it, plan on it and then send it down to middle management. Middle management will take this perfect solution and hand it to the folks in the trenches, who will implement it.

"The good news is that you've done some homework and you have a taste for what works and what doesn't. Unfortunately, this is a factory-centric approach, and in a fluid industry (which industry is no longer fluid?) it's just not going to work."

I explained this to my friends at Environmental Defense and then went on with my dichotomy.

"What if we looked at it differently? What if it looked like this?

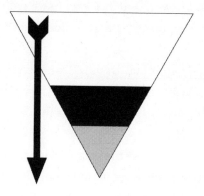

"It's not even 'bottom-up,' because that implies that the place the work gets done is the bottom. It's just reversed. Reversed in that we run the business around the tests, not the other way around. The tests aren't a sideshow that happens in the factory— the factory is a sideshow that makes our tests work better.

"What if you spent that money building a system that made it easy to test the important things and then pass the data along? Instead of speccing a rigid technical system, Environmental Defense could organize around the idea that whatever works online needs to be leveraged right now, because tomorrow it might not work online anymore."

I was gratified to see my hosts jump right on the idea. Adam, a key player in their web group, started drawing circles on top of my picture in his notebook. "So, instead of having just one or two small groups of people working on our online offers, we could open it up to hundreds of individuals or groups who want to help us succeed."

He got it exactly right. If Environmental Defense starts treating the process of finding money and activists online the same way

Linux treats their operating system, they will have a faster, more efficient process for building their organization. They would create a system that will cost them a fraction of what it would cost to guess the right answer, build an expensive database (that step alone takes a year), discover that it didn't work and then start again.

Instead, Environmental Defense can describe the building blocks (this site acquires members, this site is designed to build interactions with activists) and then pass the data and metrics one step up the hierarchy.

At the next level, management can decide which strategies are working and invest more assets in them. They can also broker relationships between the different assets. Say, for example, that the fundraising group knows that it can solicit activists for donations, but they also know through testing that 10 percent of those solicited not only don't give money, they cease being activists. By understanding these relationships, Environmental Defense can make smart decisions about which assets to use and which ones to invest in.

As new tactics and techniques surface from the relentless use of testing and fast feedback loops, the system will change. Over time, it will become something quite unlike the system they start with. Environmental Defense will evolve, with management defining the goal and the system itself morphing constantly to become more efficient.

If, on the other hand, Environmental Defense invests a big chunk of their budget in a software system, they'll be beholden to it. Working or not, it will become their winning strategy.

It's not necessarily cheaper to build a company with an evolving strategy, but it will always generate better results. That's because "I don't know" is the only true thing you can say about the future.

Because they're building their system around "I don't know," they are guaranteed that they'll be right. Testing is the heart

---

"'I don't know' is the only true thing you can say about the future."

---

of the process, not a sideshow, or a distraction or a risk. Whatever works, Environmental Defense will do that more.

Environmental Defense got it. They saw that they can't manage change, but that they can make themselves far more receptive to being managed by change. The tactics they implement are not nearly as important as their realization about change.

The Über Strategy?

Michael Porter, guru of strategy at the Harvard Business School, has pointed out that the New Economy isn't that new, and that the old strategies are just as important as (if not more important than) they ever were before. At one level, he's correct. No one has suspended the laws of economics.

On the other hand, all corporate strategy has been based on one fundamental assumption: *We can predict the future and influence its course through our actions.* It doesn't pay, after all, to have some fancy strategy that's based on a combination of competitive threats, technological innovation and government regulation if you don't believe that those three things are actually likely to happen.

The role of zooming in strategy is simple. It's based on the idea that you don't know what's going to happen. Thus, a new, overriding strategy is now laid on top of all your other strategies. This über strategy is simple: Build a company that's so flexible and responsive, both in the long term and the short term, that we don't care what happens. As long as there's a lot of noise and disorganization and change, we'll win.

In today's world, betting on chaos seems to me to be the safest bet of all.

THE IMPORTANT QUESTIONS

One way to start implementing these ideas is to ask some hard questions. Here are questions that can start you, your group and your company on the way to building a zooming organization, one that can adapt and respond rather than react to change.

Why?

Repeatedly asking this simple question is the fastest way to understand a company's winning strategy. When a manager tells you that you can't do something, ask it. Then ask it again in response to her answer. And repeat the question until you've gotten to the core meme, the basic truth that runs your business. And if that truth is no longer true, it's time to change your winning strategy.

How do you respond to small, irrelevant changes?

If corporate management decided to change everyone's title, or the arrangement of the parking spaces or the voice mail system, would your staff go nuts, or would it be business as usual? Are there union rules or longstanding policies that make changing just about anything a big deal? Organizations that have trouble zooming often have trouble with the tiny changes.

How many people have to say "yes" to a significant change?

One of the reasons intrapreneurship rarely works is that larger companies can't resist setting up committees. It only takes one person to say no, of course, but how many people have to say "yes" before a change can occur?

Here's a great idea: appoint a CNO—chief no officer. No longer can someone say no to an idea and leave it at that. If you want to turn something down, you've got to pass it on to your boss. Then either he says yes or gives it to his boss. For a no to be official, it's got to be approved by the chief no officer and countersigned by every manager along the way.

Do you have multiple projects in development that bet on conflicting sides of a possible outcome?

Companies like to take a stand, to have a point of view, to somehow will the future to turn out the way they'd like it to. How often does your company say, "We have no idea what's going to happen, so let's plan on both outcomes."

Are you building the five elements of an evolving organization?

- Evolving organizations increase their zoomwidth daily.

- They allow their employees to build quick and cheap prototypes.

- They are aware of their winning strategy and they farm and hunt it regularly.

- They instantly communicate learning across the organization so that winning memes are incorporated and bad ones are discarded.

- They practice aggressive sexual selection strategies, firing bullies with the same zeal they hire new employees.

Are you investing in techniques that encourage fast
memetic evolution?

In times of change, some companies evolve faster than others.
Here are the top ten tactics for companies that want to evolve
quickly:

1. Invest in exploring to find the memes most likely to give you success.

2. Invest extra resources taking care of the people who carry the best set of memes.

3. Create lots of memes and kill the ones that fail.

4. Recognize that monogamy is bad.

5. Have a short gestation period and high periodicity—use fast feedback loops.

6. Invest as little as possible in the act of creating each new meme—keep your overhead tiny.

7. Don't spend a lot of resources supporting memes that don't make your company more fit, regardless of how historically cherished they are.

8. Swap memes with others.

9. Depend on recombination more than mutation.

10. Feed your young—invest in the memes that are worth spreading.

What does someone need to do to get fired?

Is it easier to have a long career at your company if you keep your
head down, don't make waves and slow things down? Or do people face more career risk if they charge their way from project to
project, experimenting and often failing? If it's the former, is it
surprising that your company is so slow?

*Who are the three most powerful people standing between things
that need to change and actual action by your company?*
If you really needed to make a change to your organization—
needed to find a way to avoid a slow death by changing your winning strategy—who would oppose you?

What if you fired those people?
Now, consider what the long-term costs to the organization might
be if you just fired those people and hired replacements who
didn't have a winning strategy to defend.

What's your company's winning strategy?
Do you know what you're busy defending? Until everyone understands what your organization is currently profiting from, employees may be defending the wrong strategy! Describing your
strategy and then exposing its weaknesses will enable you to
change the parts that need changing without worrying about irrelevant sacred cows.

*Is each manager required to have her staff spend a portion of their
time on creating the future?*
Do most middle managers supervise employees who do nothing
but react to the outside world? Are they all so busy being efficient
that they have no time to become more efficient by farming? Can
they be taught to respond, or even better, to initiate?

Are you (personally) a serf, a farmer, a hunter or a wizard?
What is your personal mDNA like? How are you developing it and
where do you want it to go?

What about the people you work with every day?
Who are you having sex with at work? Are you absorbing their
mDNA or are they absorbing yours?

If you quit your job today, could you get a decent job as a farmer or a hunter?

If your organization won't let you develop your mDNA in the direction you want it to go, why not make plans to leave before the month is over? No excuses!

If you could hire anyone in the world to help your company, who would it be?

Is it Jack Welch or Bob Pittman as CEO? Or is it a brilliant research scientist for your R&D lab? Or a super salesperson to open up a new market for you? What would it be worth to have Albert Einstein in your labs? If you don't know, it's extremely unlikely that this person is just going to walk in the door and beg for a job.

What's stopping you from hiring someone that good?

People are independent actors, able to make their own decisions. If you can create an environment attractive to this person and get the word out about what a great place you're building, the kind of person you want will be more likely to show up for work next week.

If an omniscient wizard walked into your offices and described the future and told you what to do to prepare for it, would your company be able to change in response to his vision?

I'll bet you money the answer is no. Companies don't fail to change because of a lack of proof about the future. They don't change because they're stuck or they're afraid.

How can your company dramatically lower the cost of launching a test?

What's the time to market? How many hoops does someone have to go through to launch a web site or a new policy or to take a product on a sales call? At some of your competitors, it's probably one day and one approval. How hard is it at your company?

Are there five areas in your company that would benefit from fast feedback loops?
How would you measure things that you've traditionally considered unmeasurable? Can you use IT and wireless technology to start tracking things fast that others aren't tracking at all? And after you measure something, who gets the data? When?

Are you building all your systems around testing and ignorance?
It's very easy to invent the perfect system and then insist that the market and the data respond to your wisdom. It's more realistic to create a system around tests and change and evolution and let your system respond to the market.

Are you hiding from the market?
One of the short-term luxuries of a successful winning strategy is that it allows you to hide from the marketplace. A struggling entrepreneur knows about each and every missed sale. He's attuned to all of his competitors—real and imagined. When the competition starts stealing accounts, he notices it immediately.

Many successful organizations build up enough levels of insulation that they don't feel the response of the market, or, when they do feel it, it's muffled or late. In order for your feedback loops to be effective, they must be fast and appropriately tuned. That doesn't mean your entire company should freak out when a single client switches to a competitor, but it does mean that substantial criticism needs to be circulated throughout the relevant sections of the company.

Step 1: Have the president of the company answer the customer service lines for a day.

Have you ever tried sushi?

You don't have to eat it all the time. But have you ever tried it? Why not? Are you afraid? If you're afraid of food, change at work must be incredibly scary. What if you started by eliminating the hard-to-defend fears and then worked your way up?

If you could acquire another company's mDNA, whose would you choose?

Most big companies can afford to acquire one or more smaller companies. Are there companies in your industry that you admire or envy? Companies that have a better winning strategy or more attractive mDNA?

Why don't you do that?

Acquire them. If you can't, hire away a few of their employees who really "get it" and give them the resources they need to spread their mDNA through your organization. Don't bog them down with overwhelming operational responsibility that requires day-to-day reactions. Instead, let them hunt.

Are the economies of scale really as big as you think they are?

Years ago, when they built your company, it's likely that the best efficiencies came from big production runs and busy factories. A lot has changed. How much would it cost to switch to tiny batches and small efforts? Does every decision need to be a big one?

Is this project going to benefit from the learning it creates?

Most of the time, big corporate projects start with a winning strategy already defined. The feedback that comes in (from the marketplace and from the people working on the project) is ignored, or reacted to, as opposed to embraced and responded to. Is feedback on this project something to be dealt with, as opposed to being used?

In what markets could your marketing efforts enter runaway?

Where are the positive feedback loops in your business? How can you take advantage of them?

How much time does senior management spend with unhappy customers?

The farmer doesn't see a disgruntled customer the way a serf does. The factory-centric model of corporations views an angry customer as an irritant, a potential enemy of the system. A farmer, on the other hand, wants to spend as much time as possible with disappointed customers, realizing that they are a vast source of data on ways to improve the system.

What do you do with complaint letters?

Do you frame them and post them prominently? Or do you hire a low-level employee to do the minimum necessary to make the complaining person go away quietly? Perhaps you should assign them to a senior-level hunter with instructions to get the complainer actively involved instead.

What are you measuring?

Whatever gets measured is what will get done.

A fast feedback loop can't work unless you're measuring something you can change. Choosing what to measure (be specific!) is a crucial first step in evolving.

Consider a simple example from the web. Many sites continue to measure hits to their site. A hit is a vague, easily manipulated statistic, however, and it doesn't really correlate to success online. Some sites measure referrals, or clickthroughs. Others measure online orders or the response rate of prospects to e-mail. And some measure lifetime sales by customer.

Each of these measures can be justified at some level. And

choosing one of them will send your site down a very different evolutionary road than choosing another one.

Are you being selfish with your personal mDNA?

As you move through your career, loyalty is a fine tool to advance your learning. Being part of a company improves your mDNA and the best way to be part of a company is to be loyal to it. But remind yourself that every meeting, every job, every effort you make directly affects the mDNA you're building, and in the long run, just as with a gene, being selfish with your mDNA is the way you succeed.

That your genes are selfish doesn't mean you are. Often, the best strategy for a selfish gene is to cooperate.

Selfish genes are valuable because (as a side effect) they enable the organisms that house them to survive. Selfish memes are the same. The best way to grow your company is to make it a hospitable place for selfish memes and the people who carry them.

Have you institutionalized the process of sharing what you learn?

Learning that doesn't get passed on doesn't do you any good. While a dog that fetches is cute, the skill is useless to the dog species if the fetching trick doesn't get passed on to future generations. If your company is investing in farming and hunting, the effort is wasted unless you keep track and teach each other what's being learned. Remember, a selfish meme is not a private meme—the best memes spread.

Are you focusing too much?

What's the least amount of effort you need to apply to an initiative for it to have the most efficient likelihood of success? Many companies invest too much in their existing winning strategies in the mistaken belief that this investment increases the longevity of the strategy. Does it?

*Are you the first choice among job seekers who have the mDNA
you seek?*

Remember the grizzly. You don't need to be the perfect place to
work—just better than all the other options. The minute someone
with successful mDNA finds the best available job, she'll take it.
Being number two doesn't help you.

*Are you the first choice among employers that have the winning
strategy you seek?*

The same holds true for people looking for a job. Being the best
guarantees you the winner's premium, which means far more
choices and the likelihood of finding the best available job. If
you're not the best, how do you redefine the market you're hunting in so that you are the best?

What do you need to do to become the first choice?

What's the cost/benefit analysis of investing whatever it takes to
become the first choice among the best job seekers (and best
employers)? Can you create a winning strategy in which your company wins even if your employees aren't the best? How about a
personal winning strategy in which you can personally win even if
your mDNA isn't the best?

Do you zoom?

Put a z in your ads when you're hiring. Put a z on your résumé
when you're looking. It's a movement. If enough of us start to
zoom, we'll enter runaway, and then nothing can stop us.

Artificial selection When humans choose which organisms of a species they allow to breed, thus reinforcing the desired attributes in the ensuing offspring. Dogs have been artificially selected over thousands of years, giving us the Doberman and (yikes) the chihuahua. Companies can use artificial selection to intentionally evolve in a strategic direction.

Brainstorming A formal meeting process that involves bypassing the traditional criticism reflex and identifying large numbers of alternatives, regardless of their practicality. Brainstorming is difficult, not because the system is hard to understand, but because it's incredibly hard not to criticize new memes. Fighting this instinct is the essential element of any successful brainstorming tactic.

Birthing moment The shipping date for a product, the actual takeoff of a jet airliner and the first delivery of a new service are all birthing moments. These are the discrete events that separate the "we're still working on it" development stage from the "it's done" shipping stage.

Business niche Space in the competitive environment where a company can thrive. Your company has a winning strategy largely because your niche is overlooked by competitors who could crush you if they chose to. When the marketplace changes, niches are exposed, dynamics are changed and your previously safe position may be threatened.

Crispy tofu This recipe is a meme. You'll need a pound of firm tofu, cut into one-inch cubes and extremely well drained. Find the best nonstick pan in the kitchen and get it hot. Spray the pan with a Misto (or a can of Pam) filled with a blend of half sesame oil and half olive oil. Brown one side of the tofu over high heat. Flip. When the other side is browned, pour a tablespoon of soy sauce over the tofu and toss in the pan until the soy sauce caramelizes on the outside of the tofu. Serve immediately over rice.

Disposable Soma Theory The reason that genes have programmed organisms to die at a certain point is that future generations don't benefit from the same organism repeatedly reproducing. Evolution will occur faster if new generations (with new genes) are now creating the next generation.

Disposable Soma Theory (in business) Older companies with a fixed winning strategy are often replaced by entrepreneurs who discovered their (more fit) winning strategy later. If every company were directly descended from Thomas Edison's original lab, we'd have far less variation than we do now. Your business will not live forever. Your memes may, though.

DNA The molecule that carries the genetic code (the phrase is often used by laymen to include the protein effects of those genes as well). If genes are the digital data, then DNA is the storage medium.

Ecological niche Metaphorical location in the ecosystem where an organism thrives. There are obvious niches (like those inhabited by the finches in the Galápagos) and more subtle ones, like the time/altitude/weather niche of dragonflies in temperate Canada.

Entropy A law of thermodynamics that states that molecules, unless otherwise forced, become more random over time. Entropy is the reason an open container of perfume will soon stink up the entire room. Companies organize to make a profit by fighting the forces of entropy, but entropy is tireless in its quest to undo all that we do.

Evolution Heritable changes in a population spread over many generations. Species, not organisms, evolve. Human beings almost always overestimate how quickly things can change in the short run but frequently underestimate how much change can happen over time. Take a look back over the last hundred years and you can get an idea of just how much could have occurred in a period ten million times as long (a few billion years.)

Evolutionary biology The study of how evolution affects living organisms.

Farmers Employees who use testing and rapid cycle time to continually improve the winning strategy of a company. Farming is at the heart of most companies—enough farmers can create predictable improvements to a winning strategy and build the barriers to your ecological niche that can create profits for years.

Fast feedback loop A system where an employee or his company gets easily measured and very quick data about the effectiveness of a new tactic. Making a change in a web banner can create demonstrable results in just a few minutes. Fast feedback loops encourage organizations to make frequent small adjustments, making it more likely that they will farm (and evolve) their winning strategy.

Fecundity Having the attribute of fertility. New markets can be as fecund as a rainforest.

Fitness Lifetime reproductive success of an individual organism. This has nothing to do with whether one organism is "better" than another. It merely keeps score of whether an organism is more likely to survive and breed. "Survival of the fittest" is a tautology— if you survive, you're more fit.

Fitness (in business) Likelihood of success of a corporation from a particular winning strategy (success could be profits, employees hired, memes spread). Again, a company can be despicable but still fit.

Fittest When two organisms compete for an ecological niche, the winner is, by definition, the fitter. Fittest doesn't mean perfect. It just means better.

Gene The basic building block of an organism. The functional unit of heredity. Genes are data—tiny digital flags that tell proteins and other elements of the organism how to develop.

Gene pool The variations available to a species through random mating.

Genetic A trait that is heritable and hardwired into an organism.

Genomics The study of genes and their function.

Heritable In general, traits that are passed down from parent to offspring. Specifically in evolutionary biology, it refers to the percentage of a given trait that can be attributed directly to genetic transmission from parent to offspring. Most of what an employee does is not heritable, and it's the job of a successful company to figure out how to spread those memes from one employee to another.

Hotwash A detailed, no-holds-barred post-mortem, held immediately after a test of a meme.

Hunters Employees who work to expand a company's winning strategy using a wide variety of techniques. Hunters identify new markets, create new uses for old products and aggressively test new techniques for finding and keeping customers.

Length of generation Amount of time between births. Fruit flies reproduce with a very short generation, while humans take more than fifteen years to have their first child. Organizations with a long length of generation (which I call slow periodicity) are likely to evolve more slowly.

mDNA The sum of all the memes and assets (brands, factories, talented people, partners, patents, etc.) in an organization. Memes are not as digital as genes—sometimes a meme is tied up in the person or asset it inhabits and can't be easily transferred.

Meme The basic building block of an idea or organizational construct. The functional unit of idea transference. The recipe for crispy tofu is a meme. So is the idea that the world is round.

Memeplex A more complex meme that is made up of many smaller memes.

Meme pool The business variations available to a company. When a wizard invents a new meme (like selling greeting cards) that meme becomes available to anyone who chooses to take it from the pool.

Memetic evolution The change in ideas over time, as they spread from person to person and combine with other memes. The most fit memes survive and spread and combine with other memes. Unfit memes disappear.

Muller's Ratchet The continual decrease in fitness of an asexual species due to accumulation of mutations. Without sex, defective, mutated genes are passed on from generation to generation.

Muller's Ratchet (in business) The continual decrease in fitness of an organization due to the accumulation of mutations that come from hiring only people who agree with you and working only for clients who don't push you. Without sex, superstitions are passed on as tested winning strategies.

Mutation Error in the transmission of genetic information. Usually deleterious to the organism, but occasionally leading to a positive change. While it's likely that many evolutionary breakthroughs came as the result of positive mutations, most are failures.

Mutation (in business) Abrupt change in the memetic information in a company's winning strategy. Companies are far more likely to profit from the recombination of successful memes than they are from waiting for a positive mutation to occur.

Natural selection Only fit animals live long enough to reproduce.

Natural selection (in business) Only fit winning strategies allow companies to continue to hire people and raise money.

Parasite An organism that feeds on and is sheltered by a different organism while contributing nothing to the survival of its host. A flea is a parasite.

Periodicity Analogous to generations in organic evolution, a company's periodicity is an indicator of how quickly it can invent a new set of memes, install them into an organization and then expose them to the market for testing.

Positive feedback loop A system where a change in one variable causes a change in another variable, which in turn further changes the first variable. For example, eating fried foods in great quantities makes you fat, which in turn increases your desire for more fried food, which just makes you fatter.

Red Queen The competitive change in the ecosystem created by the responses of other species to a species' evolution and the co-evolution that change creates.

Red Queen (in business) The competitive change in the marketplace created by the responses to one company's evolution and the coevolution that change creates.

Resistance to mutation Species have evolved to clean up most mutations because susceptibility to mutation often leads to non-advantageous results.

Resistance to mutation (in business) Companies create handbooks and policies to avoid the unchecked spread of mutations. At the same time, organizations that resist mutation as a matter of course are at a disadvantage over those that intelligently screen out the obviously nonadvantageous mutations and test the rest.

Runaway Rapid evolution that comes when a positive feedback loop exists between sexual selection and inheritance. Coined by Sir Ronald Fisher. Peacock feathers, moose antlers and possibly human brains all evolved as a result of runaway.

Runaway (in business) Rapid evolution that occurs when a company is able to find new employees who reinforce its winning strategy of zooming. Also, rapid growth that comes from entering a market first with an offering that finds new customers who reinforce its leadership position. If you view your organization as a single entity in isolation, this makes no sense. However, when we see a company as a group of people interacting with other people, it's fairly obvious.

Serfs Employees who want to be told what to do.

Sexual selection Many species have rules regarding the way organisms choose a mate. When these rules influence the long-term evolution of the species, sexual selection is at work. For example, if the female of a species tends to choose the tallest available male, then the species is likely to become taller over time. While natural selection is an obvious driver of evolution, it may be sexual selection that is responsible for many unique characteristics of certain species, including the size and power of the human brain.

Sexual selection (in business) Many companies have rules regarding the way they choose employees to hire and fire. These rules inevitably influence the evolution of the organization, demonstrating the power of sexual selection in the workplace. Choosing whom to hire (and whom to fire) is the single most effective way most companies can create change over time.

Signaling devices Cues that communicate one organism's fitness to a potential mate or competitor.

Signaling devices (in business) Cues that communicate a company's fitness to a potential employee or customer or competitor.

Species Organisms that can successfully breed with each other to produce offspring which can still breed with each other.

Species (in business) A company is not just an organism, nor is it just a species. It's both. This is confusing (sorry). When a company conducts business as usual and uses its existing mDNA, it acts like an organism. When a company evolves by hiring or firing or expanding or shrinking or acquiring or willfully changing its mDNA, it becomes a descendant of itself, part of the same species but a new, different and maybe better organism. A company viewed over time is actually a series of organisms. Every day (or every month) its mDNA is altered substantially enough that it ceases to be that organism and starts to be this one. And when that happens, the old organism disappears and is replaced by a similar one—a new one, but part of the same species.

Stuck winning strategy A company has evolved to the point where it has so embraced its winning strategy that it doesn't have the desire, the tools or the people to find a new one.

Supply chain The employees, suppliers and distributors who work on a product from the raw materials to the final purchase.

Variation Organisms (and companies) with similar genes (and memes) still exhibit differences in their appearance and behavior.

Winning strategy The memes that make a company fit.

Wizards Employees who are able to create memes that can dramatically change a company's winning strategy.

Zoom Embracing change (causing it and responding to it) as a successful winning strategy.

Zoomers Employees who zoom.

Zoometry The study of mDNA.

THE FIELDS OF memetics and sexual selection are not without controversy. In order to present a cogent metaphor, I've played a little fast and loose with some of the details. Here, for example, is Aaron Lynch's definition of a meme: "A memory item, or portion of an organism's neurally-stored information, identified using the abstraction system of the observer, whose instantiation depended critically on causation by prior instantiation of the same memory item in one or more other organisms' nervous systems." I hope you'll agree that this level of detail would not have made it easier for me to make my point!

As I pointed out in Chapter 2, I'm not completely sold that memes are a perfect analogy for genes, but I think that the quality of the analogy is beside the point. The concept of memes makes it far easier to understand how ideas spread and how organizations establish their belief systems, and that's reason enough to include them. For those interested in a more rigorous discussion of the many scientific issues touched upon in this book, I commend you to the bibliography/reading list available by writing to books@zoometry.com.

More

You can get a complete bibliography and reading list by mailing to
books@zoometry.com.

For an updated chapter to this book, visit
www.zoometry.com/update.

To inquire about speaking engagements, please mail
dle@greatertalent.com.

This book is available at a discount for bulk purchases.
Ask at your local bookseller or write to
bulk@zoometry.com.

I answer all my mail and I'd love to hear your thoughts.
seth@zoometry.com.

Acknowledgments

I N "THE LITTLE RED HEN," no one wanted to help the hen until she'd already finished baking her bread. Writing a book can be that way as well—you understand who your real friends are when you ask someone to read an early draft!

I have to take full responsibility for any errors or inanities contained herein, but unlike previous books, this one went through many cycles. I'm grateful to Lisa DiMona, Robin Dellabough, Karen Watts, Lynn Gordon, Lisa Gansky, Beth Polish, Susan Cohen, Barbara Johnson, Thornton May, Jerry Colonna, Eve Yohalem, Jonathan Sackner-Bernstein, Alex Godin and my wife, Helene, for reading and commenting on many, many versions of this book. Paul Ryder took the time to send me pages of thoughtful questions on several of the early drafts and forced me to tighten up the science as well. Some of the most surprising and useful feedback came from Tamsin Braisher and Neil Gemmell in New Zealand—the Net is a wonderful thing. Linda Carbone did a great job of reviewing draft number seven as well. Stuart Krichevsky provided insight, support and kharmic goodwill from the very start.

Alan Webber is the finest editor I've ever worked with, and the snippets from this book that were in *Fast Company* benefited from his remarkable skill. There's no doubt in my mind that I never would have written this book or the last if *Fast Company* hadn't been the Red Queen, constantly raising the bar and pushing us to think faster and more creatively. Together with Bill Taylor, they've created not just a magazine, but a movement.

Fred Hills and his team at the Free Press have confounded my skepticism about traditional publishers. He's a great person to work with—I wish I were always this lucky.

As important as the people I actually interacted with to write this book, there are a dozen writers and thinkers who gave me the foundation to start with. Daniel Dennett, Richard Dawkins, Susan Blackmore, Chris Meyer, E. O. Wilson, Geoff Miller, Colin Tudge, Jared Diamond, Matt Ridley, and most especially, Tom Peters and Charles Darwin. If you do one thing after reading this book (other than telling all your friends) I hope that you will go read some books about evolution. They're fascinating and surprisingly useful. If you send me an e-mail at books@zoometry.com, I'll send you a list of my favorites.

For contact information on some of the people listed above, feel free to drop a line to credits@zoometry.com. These people are very good at what they do, and if you and they can profit from working together, that's great with me. Thanks.

For more information, visit these sites:

http://www.zoometry.com
to learn more about *Survival Is Not Enough*, including a bibliography and additional material. You can also find zoomwear and links for further reading, bulk sales, and speaking engagements.

http://content.monster.com/zoom
to learn more about finding a better job—a job where you're encouraged (and expected) to zoom. Or to find an employee who wants to zoom. This site also provides original articles by Seth Godin on new trends in zooming.